CLASH

NON-FICTION

Troy, NY
CLASH Books
clashbooks.com

NON-FICTION

Gender / Fucking

the pleasures and politics of living in a gendered body

———————————————

Florence Ashley

Table of Contents

To all my lovers

Preface

It is raining in the quadrangle. The thunder claps to the sound of my fingers against the keys. It scares me, unsettles me. I wish someone was holding me through it. Pausing my keystrokes, I rest my chin in my hands, my elbows on the antique table. I have long aspired to the smuttiness of *Dungeon Intimacies*, Susan Stryker's essay on the "poetics of transsexual sadomasochism." Reading it aroused me(,) as I learned. Although I have slipped the occasional pearl-clutching footnote into articles, none were so openly erotic. Academic smut should be a recognized genre. It merges two of the things that make me horny— theory and sex. In that order.

We might benefit from taking intellectual masturbation a bit more literally. Some truths can only be told through the erotic. Polaroid captures of the messiness of life in its rawest forms. There's so little appreciation for the knowledge that comes with arousal. We instead associate it with unthought, with primal urges that override our ability to understand and reason. Grand welcomes for pluralities of genre and polyepistemologies; for the autoethnographic and phenomenological and all the novel ways of knowing, yet so few praises for erotica. So few praises for bodily epistemologies—unless they are abstracted beyond recognition. Ever fewer among the academically inclined. Though they may be far more welcoming than their disciplinary cousins, even in queer and trans studies does prudishness occasionally shine through. Smut has been relegated to fanfiction and self-published novels, as though it were an art without teaching. Not even an art—a craft. Craft is the name of derided arts. But all arts are crafts, all crafts are art. If I had to describe my book, that's what I would call it. Academic smut. A web from interweaved strands of sex, speculation, messiness, and camp. Would it even be queer without a bit of purple?

My essays attempt to put the sex back in transsexual, as it were. That's perhaps more pun than wisdom. When I joked at a workshop that I would write a text with that title, Viviane Namaste reminded me that it had never left. She is right— we are a horny bunch. I can't even count the number of trans academics I've traded nudes with, nor the number of dates that began in a direct message on social media. Yet I cannot deny that de-sexualized undercurrents have risen to the surface of trans advocacy. Pages were taken from Victorian prudishness. I understand, somewhat. Between the doctrines of autogynephilia—we are trans because we are confused, perverted straight men—and androphilia—we are trans because we are extra gay—dissociating sex from transitude holds a certain appeal. We are no longer transsexual, because transitude has naught to do with sex. It's all gender, baby. Plus, y'know, binariness and medicalization and all that distasteful jazz.

Chatting online with me, Leah Tigers spoke of how pursuing *more* sexuality would be a deeply misguided response when sexualization is one of the primary vectors of trans people's oppression—sexualization in its most original, primordial, and nocturnal sense. If we are autogynephiles, evil deceivers, predators, rapists—is that not already a surplus of sexuality? How could we possibly want more?

She has a point. Yet at the very same time as we are sexualized, we are also desexualized. We are undesirable, disgusting, mutilated. We are unfit for marriage and parenthood; forced into divorce, sterilized. Trans lives are lived at a critical juncture of de/sexualization; depicted as hypersexual precisely to shame us into divesting from sex. An uneasy duality reminiscent of women's pathologization for both wanting and not wanting sex; of the misogynoir that sees Black women simultaneously hypersexualized and degendered, facing the dual stereotypes of Jezebel and Mammy; of the white supremacist, desexualizing animus underpinning Black and Indigenous women's forced sterilizations.

The double bind of de/sexualization is a resilient one, one that makes leaving its clutches only harder. Be overtly sexual and you will confirm their assumptions, justify their agenda. Suppress sexual desires and, over time, no room will be left for the sex workers, the sluts, and the perverts; for those whose sexuality is pushed to the shadows as they hunger for the liberty and safety to express it; for those who are horny for some gender*fuck*. Oppression thrives in double binds. Neither sexuality nor its absence provide a satisfactory answer to transmisogyny—we need both.

This book takes the sex path, not to apotheosize it but rather to capture its earthly messiness. It attempts to capture my communion with the erotic, to capture some of what I have learned from its depths. Perhaps it is a love letter to messiness, in a way. Sex is messy; that's what I love about it. It is pleasure and pain; it is ambivalent, ambiguous. It is human—part of the multiplicity in our beings that does not, should not be singled out for severance from those of us who house it. Sexuality is not liberation, but perhaps we can learn about the path to liberation from it. I long after the words of Audre Lorde:

> In touch with the erotic, I become less willing to accept powerlessness, or those other supplied states of being which are not native to me, such as resignation, despair, self-effacement, depression, self-denial.

The erotic is embodiment, feeling. It is the light that turns inwards. *L'érotique déconstruit et reconstruit mes connaissances charnelles.* This manuscript is a diary of my innermost sexual thoughts—thoughts that are asunder, revealing the messiness inside. A messiness I hope to learn from. I wrote this instead of going to therapy.

I lust for messiness. Messiness takes on an idiosyncratic tone in my voice as I try to capture the ineffable, beautiful disorder of human life with its polychromatic emotions. Tortuous, sinuous, intricate—like the cushiony web of a black widow, like the mesmerizing chaos of a strange attractor. Messiness is neither good nor bad—it is beautiful. Emotional monochrome may be simple, but it is ugly.

At the juncture of the messiness of gender and sexuality is gender/fuck. At once gender, fuck, and genderfuck, the juxtaposition speaks of the political element in exploring and revealing gender through sexuality and sexuality through gender. Balancing out the medical and exclusionary resonances of the word 'transsexual,' genderfuck rejects neoliberal modes of living and attempts to discipline and standardize gender. In acknowledging that both gender and sexuality are fundamentally and irreducibly political experiences, gender/fuck gestures toward community—dare I say, *cum*munity—acknowledging that my inner world is infinitely reproduced in others. Gender and sex are not lonely worlds. They are relational, even when masturbating. We all share in bodily knowledge; always unique, always same. The erotic vignettes that populate my essays only reveal my inner world; others in my sexcapades have theirs, just as real as mine, even if I could not see it. But if I narrate my own, perhaps I can create and hold space for others'.

The erotic vignettes that adorn these pages were written at various points in my life, about various points in my life. Most are composites of what has occurred; some are strictly faithful to experience; some interweave lies conjured for narrative purposes. Faithful to spirit, if not word. If I knew more about literature, I might call it autofiction. Lest you think my life interesting, let me pre-emptively correct your mistake—I lead a boring life punctuated by tales.

The reflections accompanying the smut are thoughts of a messy human living in a body with its share of trauma and hang-ups. You are messy too; you have your trauma and hang-ups too. Perhaps far worse than mine. That's why I suspect my words might speak to you. You will learn far too much about my sexual life; one hopes that you will learn other things as well, but if not, then you will probably at least be entertained. I wrote for my lovers and friends. I wrote for trans folks and folks who have bodies. I wrote for all the messy people. It was therapeutic—I hope it can be for you as well.

Before you begin reading, you should be warned that I extensively discuss transphobia and transmisogyny throughout the book and that two chapters, *Permission to Hurt* and *Libidinal Vertigo*, discuss sexual violence at length. Take precautions if you need to, or skip them entirely. While the various chapters resonate with one another, they are standalone and your experience will not be irreparably diminished if you skip those two.

My preface has gone on long enough. The rain has tarried. I can smell the petrichor in the air between the faraway flashes of lightning, too far to reach my ears. I wonder if my words will come off as insightful or masturbatory. Hopefully both.

Sexually Transmissible Transitude

Pushed against the wall, blindfolded with hands tied behind my back, I could sense the tremors spread through my side into my chest as she masturbated on the bed. Her hand pressed on my back and the mattress vibrating as she brought her hand up and down, I could feel every little movement. A warmth was awash my body, a pulsating sensation of arousal that I could feel in my arms, my toes, and my genitals. Between the strokes, she would ask if I wanted to join her. She would make me beg. After a few minutes of agonizing pleas, she turned me on my back. As I rested uncomfortably atop my bound hands, I anticipated with delight her mouth on my body. As she began licking and sucking on my dick, a moment of magical transformation transpired. Unable to see, my brain abandoned its attempts at predicting my body and turned to pure feeling. In her mouth, without a word spoken, my penis became a clitoris. My taint throbbed for fingers, sensing the craving emptiness in its midst. In Charlotte's arms, I didn't have to think. I could just *be*. "Good girl," she murmured, recognizing needs I didn't yet know I had. The blood flowed to my cheeks as I stammered a response. "T- thank you, miss." I didn't know what to call her and felt my anxiety roused for a brief moment before it dissipated in a moan of pleasure, my unintentional response to the flick of her tongue. The pulsation in my every limb grew insistent, craving for the space beyond my skin that contained it. And as my moans grew ever louder, Charlotte's mouth only multiplied its ardor around my clit. I could feel the world inside me swelling to come out, my skin distended to its very limits. Until, a few moments later, I erupted onto myself. Giggling, Charlotte carried cum to my mouth with her index, repeating in a soothing tone how much of a good girl I had been and how proud of me she was as I sucked on her finger. Though I did not notice it at the time, I was overcome with abandon. Noticeably absent from my body-mind was the affect of shame and guilt that had always defined my post-orgasmic moments, before.

Years later, as I returned home, I wondered how many people I turned trans. So many people I believed to be cis men came to realize that they were trans after a few hook-ups with me, a phenomenon that seems shared among trans elders—which, these days, includes everyone who has come out more than three years ago. I'm a bit sad. It's not that I mind Dominique being trans, but she was a good lay and I hoped to continue sleeping with her. But I don't sleep with baby transes. It's too messy, too uncomfortable. Having already navigated the social and medical space of transitioning, I become a trove of information and advice for them. Their unacknowledged desire for a parental figure to guide them through the uncertainty of baby transhood is transferred onto me as an experienced someone that they have affective ties to. They want me to be their mother. Sigmund would probably have a field day theorizing about baby trans-ference.

Beyond the unhealth of symbolic incest, baby transhood returns me to a past of intense dysphoria. I survived the deadly traps of the social and medical dungeon to loot the treasure of euphoria and leave my dysphoria behind. I have little interest in revisiting that ordeal through another's body-mind. Too much of Dominique reminds me of myself then, and I hated myself. My projection of dysphoric affect onto her is unfair, but it is not one I can control. If I could, my life would have been far simpler.

I wonder if that's why Charlotte and I stopped seeing each other. I wonder if I was another egg she broke. I wonder if she resented me. I wonder if she also felt like she was nothing more than a short stop on eggs' quest to find themselves. What is it about us that attracts eggs like moths to a flame?

Over the last few years, I've been writing about the conviction among cis parents that being trans is a social contagion that has climbed to heights of pandemic proportion. I have dedicated myself to proving the fallacy of the suggestion. Writing these words, I firmly believe that they are wrong. But as I reflect on embodying t4t, I can't help but wonder whether fertile avenues of understanding may be opened up by thinking of transitude as contagious, as a sexually transmissible condition. Though I would never adopt it in my legal or bioethical scholarship, I suspect it holds the seeds of a poetic, affective truth. I fuck, date, and love trans girls. I fuck, date, and love trans girls even when neither of us knows we are. I love them before they come out, holding open the possibility that every cis person is in a state of becoming toward transitude. I love them so much, I *make* trans girls. It may not be quite true, but I feel it in my bones.

A tattoo on the back of my neck reads t4t. I had it

drawn after reading Torrey Peters' *Infect Your Friends and Loved Ones*. Although I may eschew transbian separatism—the abuses of radical lesbianism and of bæddelism standing as warnings—Torrey's aspirational t4t philosophy spoke to me:

> You just promise to love trans girls above all else. The idea—although maybe not the practice—is that a girl could be your worst enemy, the girl you wouldn't piss on to put out a fire, but if she's trans, you're gonna offer her your bed, you're gonna share your last hormone shot. […] We aim high, trying to love each other and then we take what we can get. We settle for looking out for each other. And even if we don't all love each other, we mostly all respect each other.

There is both a promise and a danger to t4t. It carves a space for liberation outside of cisgender society, knowing that safety and self-worth are rarely attainable within its reaches. It posits that, however dangerous they can be, transfeminine arms will not misrecognize us. And it delights in ridiculing the transantagonistic claim that trans girls wouldn't date other trans girls and, thus, disprove themselves as proper subjects of lesbian lust. Yet too must the danger be emphasized. In our trauma, we are often quick to lash out at each other. In our trauma, we often refuse to let ourselves be lovable to cis people, not because we believe trans love is revolutionary but because we don't think we are good enough, lovable enough. Trans love shouldn't be a consolation prize.

Is what I brought to Dominique the same thing that Charlotte brought me? I longed for her touch. I delighted in how she knew my body-mind better than I did and unearthed the love I held for it. I cannot resent her for turning away from me. By unfurling trans knowledges in my body, she felt that she made me as I am. She is connected to my fate; she began a pattern in it, tying herself to my future joys and pains. Like Charlotte to me, I to Dominique. I transmitted my transitude to her. If she rejoices, my heart may swell. But what if she does not. What if she, like too many of us, takes her own life? In poetry, being trans is a sexually transmissible condition. That may be too large a burden for us to bear.

Do you remember when you were scared to wear nail polish to work? Do you remember how you told me you felt so badass? Do you remember when you sent me pictures with this pink nail polish on, and the little blue accent nail? Do you remember when you were still alive?

Trespass on the Fox

We met on the curb in front of Peel Pub, that college dive bar down the street from the faculty. Apprehensive of mistaken identities, I ignored the figure on the sidewalk until he waved me over. I must have looked like a lumpy lighthouse with my white shirt and bright red hair. I always let my dates find me; my anxiety won't let it be otherwise. Tucking the temple of my shades in my waistband, I threw my right hand around his neck and kissed his cheek. His neck smelled of Diesel perfume, you know, the one that looks like a masturbating fist. Perching over me as we hugged, he made me feel small—a rare, precious feeling given how tall I am. Even though we'd only briefly chatted after meeting on a dating app, I'd collected hope that between the stature and the tattoos, we had enough supplies for a pleasant if ephemeral moment.

During my brief semester of college and then law school, I never would've thought of going to Peel Pub when the campus bar was right there. But then again, I never would've thought to fuck a business student, yet here we are. Following him inside, I sat on the chair he pulled for me at a table in the center of the room, away from the muted televisions playing whatever sports people play in the middle of the weekday. The rare customer glared at us as we sat down. Or, I should say, glared at *me*—perhaps wondering if my date knew I was trans. My gaze glued itself on the menu, pretending I didn't notice the stares while my date ordered us a pitcher of whatever cheapest beer was on tap.

Much of our conversation is already lost to the vagaries of time, flowing out from our table like a gust of wind dissipating as it finds higher pressure. Maybe it was unmemorable. Maybe I was just stunned by the confusing queer-straightness of being on a date with a man. Twenty years of being told liking men is gay is not something you forget in a day. Or two.

Waiting for the pitcher to arrive, he took his phone out of his jean pocket and browsed excitedly, looking for something, until his thumb came to a rest. He looked up at me, his lips ever-so-slightly parted, as if about to blurt out some scandalous secret. Scooching sideways to hide his phone under the line of sight of the table—I guess he *did* notice people gawking—he whispered a little too loud that the video already playing before my eyes was of his friend blowing three straight guys in an alley. The friend's gloating about his oral prowess had apparently piqued their curiosity. "Men are rarely as straight as they purport to be," my date told me. I don't know if he meant that as a confession. A scandalous, uncomfortable secret from a 'straight' guy trying to woo a woman to bed. You could almost hear me mentally clutching my pearls as my cheeks filled with a reddish hue. My feelings tantalized, pinned between arousal, unease, and fear, thoughts coursed chaotically through my brain, fighting for brief flashes of attention. Am I okay with seeing this? What if other customers see us? What if the waitress comes back with our pitcher? Why is he showing me this? A power thing? Isn't he straight? Did the impromptu actors consent to being filmed or, worse, paraded by friends of the lascivious stranger?

Maybe I should have gone home then. And I did, not long after—my date in tow and a pit in my stomach. I don't know if it was arousal or unease. I don't know if there's a difference.

"I wonder if I have him blocked on Twitter," I

wondered as I read the ramblings of the self-styled transamorous man published in the *Transgender Studies Quarterly.* Finishing, one descriptor imposed itself upon my mind: masturbatory, in more than one sense of the term. The essay struck an unusually uncritical chord on the relationship between cis men and trans women—especially those working in pornography and other parts of the sex industry. Unusually—for a scholarly journal comfortably steeped in critical theory and taking pride in fighting against "the objectification, pathologization, and exoticization of transgender lives." Uncritical— because of the essay's all-too-casual dismissal of the possibility of fetishism when, week in and week out, I find myself blocking men after they retweet my bland selfies alongside swathes of pornographic videos and photos, under the panoptic gaze of their erection-*cum*-profile picture. Two summers ago, a friend even came upon my selfies on a porn website—my face and unlicensed masturbatory stock photos, they're the same picture.

Under the cover of anonymity, doubtless many of my lustful followers would sport the 'transamorous' label. Their relationship to transfeminine bodies structured by eroticization, I have come to know them as 'chasers.' There is probably a fine metaphor to be made with their metonym. Something about their discreet pace in the shadow, the terror sparking in our bambi eyes—although I guess *Fleur* is the trans one in that movie—and the feast they make out of our bodies. I was taught that they do not love transfeminine people, that they would not dare be seen in public with me. I was taught that they do not love us; they fuck us. We are creatures. Like meat, we are disposable. At least, that's what I was taught.

After manually blocking 900-something cis men who turned the most mundane captures of my life into objects of sexual consumption, I struggle to trust cis men. Not all grizzlies, but this fawn would never. I struggle to trust cis men when walking down the street means threatening yells and objects thrown at my body, at the very same time as another dinged my phone with 'that's hot.' What fawn would ever? They told me they love my cock, not even knowing it is only ever flaccid. I don't know how to begin trusting cis men when they tell me they love me, that they aren't chasers, that they don't fetishize me, that they only have a healthy, respectful preference. What about my broad shoulders, my soft scruff, my drooping tummy? Do you love them too?

It is not that I distrust men so much as I *dys*trust them. My distrust is shapely in its inescapable wedding to the dysphoric hypersexualization of phallic female forms *qua* other, *qua* never-quite-female. Dysphoric distrust or trust that dysphoria shall come? 'That's hot,' echoes the woman who excitedly invited me to play in-between to her female self and male friend, with her tone that said I would not dare say no, that her desire was a gift. The chaser gaze finds my transfeminine body enticing *because* it can never be female—and not because I am non-binary, since I wasn't back then. No. It can never be female to them because it is the gender in-betweenness that makes me taboo and, thus, arousing. The day trans women become women in the eyes of society is the day the chaser ceases to be. I am not sure I want to be a stepping-stone in not-so-straight men's journey of sexual self-discovery. This isn't to say that attraction to trans women is gay—but it is to posit that chaserdom and straightness might just be mutually exclusive.

Awash in dystrust, transamory is not something I can believe in. They are all chasers. If not in essence, then at least in nature; if not in actuality, then at least in potentiality. That's the problem with dystrust. It knows no distinction between chaserdom and transamory. Even from flawless words, a man attracted to me breeds dystrust. My emotion projects itself into the world, spreading like a neurotoxin. My dystrust *makes* men chasers—not literally but metaphorically, by depositing in every soul the seed of chaser gaze and, along with it, a dysphoric potential. Without the curio, the fetish, the misgendering, is it possible for a cis man to love a woman *because* she is trans—rather than *despite*? My guts tell me their love is lust. Their sweat smells of lust. Their cum tastes of it. A venomous lust—a sting soon followed by dysphoric anaphylaxis. Kissing them, I feel like a white-tailed deer raising her head at grass ruffling in the wind, not knowing if I'm about to get shot, mauled, or caressed by the cooling air. My senses have led me astray before.

Arched over the pillow, I can feel my fox plushie's judging eyes on the bookshelf. Telepathically, its soft voice echoes in my head, yipping, don't I know better. His tone reminds me of the shallow cuts in my forearms, how they reverberated in my girlfriend's voice like she was unaware I was hurting. Self-harm and sex meld like copper and zinc in a furnace. They make the most beautiful sound. Pain is erotic.

A hand plunges toward my ass, my body jerks under the blow. I wince. "What a beautiful creature," he mutters as he traces the surface of my pulsing skin with the tip of his finger. Like a copper wire, place too much voltage on my nerve endings and they catch fire. But instead of smoke, it's adrenalin washing off, drowning out the endorphins—a promise of greater pain to come. Lifting and flogging down, his palm crosses over that threshold. My lower eyelid swells. I can feel the pressure building at that point just above my nose. But I don't want him to stop; I don't tell him. I want him to want me, to *need* me. And he does. I want to be wanted, after being loathed by men just like him. Maybe him, too, when he's walking down the streets with his boys.

Use me. Inscribe the sexiness in my bones. Teach me that it's not a pathetic lie I made up with my castaway friends. Take me, primally, viscerally. Desire me so utterly that you weep from the realization that your hunger can never be sated. The feeling that you can never be close like beads of water meeting as they dance on glowing steel, I want it to course through your body as you eat me, forgetting the difference between sex and brutality—too shared in their primality to differ. Use me. Ransack my body. Use me like I want to use you. You are my validation. *Quid pro quo.*

He whispers in my ear, I nod obediently. His belt comes off the hoops of his jeans, and he carefully but confidently wraps it around my neck. It can't be his first time. His belt is of faux leather, one of those punk belts with parallel holes all around. He fits the belt loosely around my throat, a makeshift collar. The hanging part of the belt looped around his left hand, he pulls himself inside me. My arms give under me and I fall on the bed face first, weak from the throbs against my prostate. Collared, I belong for a brief moment.

I write this vignette as I sit topless at my desk on a Sunday afternoon, overlooking the inner courtyard of the college. Stuck in the middle of a pandemic, inside alone with my memories, a hand down the panties I ordered online last week. I hear laughter and fountains through my window as I reminisce about having a dick—uncertain if I hated it or thought it cute, all pink and soft.

What is a chaser but a man? A man of particular cloth, flavor, regimen. A fuckboy with a lime twist. When patriarchal sexuality makes a province out of sexual objectification, perhaps all attraction is fetishism. When I was a young boy, my father took me into the city to see movies filled with tales that cast heterosexual romance as a chase. On the screen, romance meant ignoring women's desires long enough that they relented. Casual sex was the outcome of 'chasing tail.'

Men are predators. Women are their prey. Women are the unknowable, fabled creatures materialized in men's primal dreams. You know, the ones that have you wake up sticky. Womanhood is treated as a commodity to be possessed and accumulated, sexuality a mere continuation of the logics of capital. It sure sounds like men aren't supposed to *like* women. Wives are balls and chains; sport is made out of teasing men for the shameful, shameful shame of enjoying their girlfriend's company—so *whipped*. And if you want to fap to anything other than penile intercourse with a conventionally attractive cishet white woman, you'll have to head on over to a special category—one that rarely boasts a flattering let alone respectful title. Chasers have treated our transfeminine bodies poorly, to be sure, but the difference seems of degree, not kind. Thinking back to the men my friends warned me about, often too late, I am unsure how to distinguish chasers from mere men. Perhaps there can be no womanlier treatment than being fetishized.

Do you remember *Pierson v. Post*? An empty beach near Southampton, New York, 1802. Lodowick Post and his hounds were in hot pursuit of a fox, certain it would soon be his. A saucy intruder, Jesse Pierson, seeing the fox intercepted it. With his gun, shot it and carried it away to do with its pelt and carcass as he pleases. For his grave defiance of the rules of gentlemanly hunting, he was met with a lawsuit. I learned about the case in law school, where they used to teach us the social construction of ownership. Convention defines possession, a convention of control. Yet the New York Supreme Court of Judicature read convention not in the mores of the community, but in the quills and fountain pens of Justinian the Great and Henry de Bracton; in the forlorn pages of the *Fleta*. A convention of the dead—how suiting.

Between the sportsmanlike hunter and the saucy intruder, the fox is no less dead. Chasers may not abide by the same rules of the game, but they are playing the same sport—fetish is only the name we give to desires disenfranchised. Disenfranchisement comes with its share of undesirables—entitlement, fear, shame, *danger*. But the rest is just the same bad, selfish sex. Re-reading *Pierson v. Post*, all I notice is how little the difference between chasers and men matters to the fox. "Grab 'em by the girldick," says Donald Trump.

For the hurt they cause, my dismissal of men who prefer transfeminine bodies comes easy. Falling into the trappings of Manichean, good-and-bad thinking comes with perhaps too great an ease. My social web uncouples me from men. Between the layers of privilege and queer t4tness, my romantic, sexual, and economic lives can flourish without men. The juncture of desires I sit atop is one that can easily dismiss desires that betray my ideals, immersed as I am in confidence that others will take their place. I don't *need* men. To forego is a meek sacrifice. Perhaps no sacrifice at all.

Chaser—a term whose toxicity flourishes in the bosoms of those who want nothing to do with cis men, of those whose dystrust echoes the ease with which they can do without them. Maybe I would not speak so ill of them if their tainted love sustained me. The unspoken assumption of a universal transfeminine experience lies shallow beneath chaser discourse, forgetting as it does the heterogeneity of transitude. Forgetting that we come to transamorous relationships in a world shaped by the confluence of racism, colonialism, ableism, transphobia, and the indomitability of love and lust. You cannot help who you love—unless, of course, it is chasers you love. How could my words ever do justice to those whose lives are intertwined with chasers, for whom 'transamory' and 'chaser' can name both pain and pleasure? No enviable curse is it, choosing between fetishization and love *in spite of*. Between welcoming a tainted embrace or yielding to a reluctant one. Dare I spit on those who desire otherly?

What hubris to judge, I who could have avoided chasers yet still fucked them. But what would be the point? Chasers may not consider trans women to be fully, *truly* women, but in this I doubt they are alone. Do lesbians? Do bisexuals? Do *we*? Is it not our shameful secret that even we sometimes misapprehend our own genders, vacillate in our conviction that we are *just as gendered* as cis people—

exception for the genderless? For all the men that have fetishized me, maybe overtness was the only distinction.

As I track the roots downwards from the tree of my dystrust and find the dangerous proclivities of cis men toward misgendering, objectification, fetishism, and intimate partner violence, I wonder if I may not also find there a seed of (self-)contempt. Every time I open a dating app lately, I wonder if I am open to being loved, to being *lovable*. The hurt I hold because of chasers is real, but in my animosity toward cis men who profess their preference for transfeminine bodies, I also discern a hint of self-hatred. There are parts of me that do not believe a cis man could truly love my transfeminine self, without their 'love' being grounded in fetish, objectification, and misgendering. So often do I feel that my full self cannot be loved because of its transitude, that the only love I could ever receive is begrudging. When I first read the eponymic transamorous man's words in *TSQ*, when I heard him speak of creatures, I was brought back to my doubts as to the possibility of authentic love for the transfeminine—love not *in spite* of transitude but *because* of it. Collapsing the space between transamory and chaserdom with the stroke of a single brush, is our dystrust in cis men, or is it dystrust in ourselves? Maybe I need to hold open the possibility of transamorous men flourishing into good partners—if not for them, then for myself.

What makes transamorous desire impossible while we idolize t4t? When we broke up, my ex-girlfriend wondered what difference there was in my exaltation of trans women, of girldick and mouthfeel, between me and chasers. Aren't I objectifying just the same? I didn't have an answer for her at the time. None better now. I am not alone in wondering when t4t becomes chaser-y. My friend Jacq Brasseur desperately hopes that they are not like a transamorous man: "I have to ask myself if there's some truth to the joke."

Maybe it says something, how we give ourselves the benefit of the doubt in t4t but rarely extend the same to transamorous men. They alone incur our dystrust. There are differences, I know, I know. Whereas chasers are othering transfeminine bodies, t4t projects self-love onto the other. By loving trans women, I am loving myself. In loving her body, I learn to see the beauty in mine. Yet even that love strikes me by its objectification—am I not using her as an instrument, a means of my own growth? Digging down inside myself, I come upon a cave. Might I be wrong that the suspicion I lack toward t4t rests on its consolatory aspects? Doubts overtake me as to the possibility of authentic cis male love because I doubt a *monstrous* body like mine is lovable, but I do not doubt the love of other trans people because somewhere deep down I suspect it's a consolation prize. *If nobody will love us, I guess we'll have to love each other.* Is loving each other nothing but a vampiric desire to make our trans bodies desirable? I am being uncharitable; I do believe in t4t love. I do believe in it without instrumentalization, without consolation. I believe in the intimacy of trans love. But as I write these words, I am also starting to believe in the possibility of transamorous love. Blossoming, flourishing love; passionate love; consuming and warming love.

To quote communist daddy G.A. Cohen, this chapter has no conclusion. There are questions without answers. Am I open to being loved, to being lovable? Maybe. I don't know if I'll ever find an answer—perhaps I should be humbler in my ignorance. Perhaps we all should. For the time being, I will wallow in my dystrust. It is all I know.

Pushing me on my back, he leans over to kiss me. His lips unlocking from mine, he whispers, asking for my cock inside him. I shake my head. "No," I cannot. Even before hormones, I struggled to stay hard enough to achieve penetration; now, an erection is more than I can muster with unperturbed concentration. "Why do men always assume I can or want to do that," I riposte in something of a mean tone. The answer is always porn, a trove of assumptions about how my body works.

As my lips close, his eyes are filled with frustration. He stammers through a disjointed response about fucking me and why couldn't I return the favor—as though the 'favor' went one way. He came inside me. Compromising—or relenting—I get up from the sheets and walk to the ajar closet. Rummaging through my toys, carefully disorganized in a cardboard box on the shelf, I brandish my red harness adorned by embroidered patterns. Its black bow dangles down my back as I adjust the straps to my ass under the watch of his subdued nods. He positions himself on his back as I strut the few meters back to the bed. The earlier spark of his enthusiasm seems missing from his umber irises.

Eyelids closed, he looks relaxed. His eyebrows are softly raised, like bushy arches framing the soft, sandy hills of his windswept eyes. I slide one, then two fingers inside him, stopping before the second knuckle. I can feel his warm exhale against my forehead, his dewy pulse against my fingertips. Adroit and deliberate, I feel almost as much of a landscaper than a lover. After his breathing steadies and the second ring stretches, I slowly pull my fingers out of him and take them to spread the lube on my silicone cock. I warm it in my palm before tucking it against his entrance and gently pushing the head inside his ass. A low, rumbling moan escapes his lips. Counting down a few seconds to let him adjust, I begin a familiar sway with my hips. Detachable is much easier to handle. But he would have preferred the creature's flesh.

i put a hex on this town
   so it will never hurt you again
with leaves and earth and decaying grass
   i cast my magick into a spell
to fill this plain we called a home
    though only on bared bones, in a field of pain
       and death
     was it made into one

witchy vibes travel like sound waves
               encompassing all
     penetrating even the hardest of stones

the crystals we keep will mark us
   etch protection onto our skin
        in a symbol only we
           can recognize

no longer will this town hurt you again
      instead of birthing daggers their eyes will
     bleed for forgiveness

a forgiveness that is only yours to give
      such is my gift to you

Wonderfully Monstrous Bodies

Riding the Metro North train back from Poughkeepsie, in view of the beautiful Hudson River, I took to thinking about bodies. Lately, I've been thinking about what it means to change my body, as I am about to have major surgery. You know, the chop chop one.

One of the very first critiques of trans women was that they were a product of a patriarchal medical establishment that sought to eradicate gender nonconformity. According to this critique, doctors didn't like the fact that people didn't conform to gender norms and decided to use medical technology to make feminine men into women and masculine women into men. Transition-related interventions were recast into terms of conformity: why couldn't we just be happy with our bodies? In those theologian feminists' eyes, we were merely instruments of the medical establishment's erasure of feminine men and masculine women, to the benefit of men. We were monstrous travesties, botched attempts at approximating aesthetic womanhood.

The accusation, of course, is wholly ridiculous. Critiques have been plentiful, with sociologist Carol Riddell's *Divided Sisterhood*, media theorist Sandy Stone's *The 'Empire' Strikes Back*, and rogue intellectual Emi Koyama's *Whose Feminism Is It Anyway?* being among the most famous ones.

My favorite one—though they are all good— remains Susan Stryker's *My Words to Victor Frankenstein Above the Village of Chamounix: Performing Transgender Rage*. Instead of shying away from the image of Frankenstein's monster emerging from the narratives of those theologian feminists, Stryker draws on the power of the metaphor to paint a kinder picture of trans lives. It is a fundamentally human picture.

Frankenstein's monster isn't just a story of medical power. It's also a story of how we, as agents in the world, have a surplus of subjectivity that cannot be constrained by the boundaries of our creation. We are able to go beyond the society that creates us, however difficult it may be.

By drawing on the figure of the monster as quintessentially human, I wish to highlight how our wonderful, beautiful monstrosity cannot be reduced to mere conformity. However we may conform, there is always going to be a part of meaning in our scars, physical and psychological, that makes us strangely human. That, to me, is sublime.

I find it peculiar
        how we talk of hormones
                and surgeries
    as though they are conforming
        our bodies

 As I await my surgery
I am confronted with the undeniable queerness
                of stitched-up bodies

Is Frankenstein's monster conforming to society
                for not being a mound of rotting flesh?

                I will always be sewn together,
        flesh-bound to be as grotesque
    as I am sublime,
        the essence of humanity
expressed in the messiness of my body

There is none more human than the monster,
    that same monster I am set on proudly becoming

The monstrosity is my humanity,
   and in this world there is little less conforming
than aspiring to be human

The Cutting Table

Our lips met as I lay on my back, their silhouette straddled over me. Our entangled bodies naked but for their binder and my socks—the gray flowery ones with frills at the ankle. Soft bedsheets bundled up against their calves. My testicles radiated in ache, wanting for me to pinch and rub the skin with my thumb. Their discomfort had grown and lingered over weeks as testosterone re-entered my bloodstream and resumed production. Even morning wood had returned.

"I love you." They pulled on my cock, bringing it to the mouth of their vagina. My erection pulled the atrophied skin taut. I longed to be inside them, a deep craving that felt at once new and familiar, like visiting my hometown and fucking in my childhood bedroom as my parents busied themselves downstairs.

"Is this okay?" I nodded, a faint smile across my

lips. Guided by their hand, they descended on my cock. A moan of satisfaction left my throat, groaning at the feeling of pleasure, of localized bliss, pumping through my dick. Their wet pussy hugging my cock down the shaft. We paused, paused to breathe in the sentiment of intimacy—as if our bodies merged, joined at the pubic mound. Their arousal against my skin and the pressure hugging my girldick obscured, for a moment, the numb pain in my corpus cavernosum brought from blood stilled, trapped in its spongy pores.

Leaning to kiss me, they began to sway up and down my cock. I threw my arms around their shoulders, resting a hand in their hair and the other against their scapula. The cyprine of their vulva pooled against my pubis, their fluid motion ever-so-slightly sticking us together with every downward thrust. The sensation of cum began to well up through my prostate, carrying a premonitory drop to my head. Penetration had long left our repertoire, yet this last time lacked the dread of permanence. Knowing it without encore, I let my body take in the feelings in quiet. My love, they were so gentle and sweet, and I, so vulnerable. Tears flowed to the corner of my eyes. I swallowed them. "I love you."

Day I. Strangers stood around me, chatting. Their

faces hidden behind masks, no doubt to prevent me from recognizing them. Yet I was not scared; they had drugged me with sedatives, leaving me in a comfortable and confident state. Confidence in the hurt to become of my body—perhaps even a moment of confidence in the state of the world. Powerful drugs, these. They inserted a large needle in my back, and I lay awake as they labored, cutting me up. The one between my legs took exception to my babbling mouth as I tried to establish a bond with one of the strange silhouettes around me. To keep me quiet, the one I had been heretofore conversing with released a fluid in the plastic tube that ran into my arm 'til I was on the brink of sleep, slipping in and out of consciousness. Though in muted whispers they spoke, I could hear their thoughts—*oh my god, will you shut the fuck up*.

They castrated me. At least, I think that's what they were doing. I faintly remember this morning, standing in front of the mirror at norm, joyfully performing a *no-mo-penis* dance. I remember an unfamiliar bathroom, peeing for the last time. I bid farewell to my floppy stick. Goodbye friend, see you on the other side. I woke up to a sterile room. My first thought was about just how well and mentally present I felt, as though I had but just napped. Their needle, the one that made me lose sensation in my lower body, was kind to my body-mind.

Waking up, the pain was intense—seven out of ten—but stabilized around three or four. The tube in my arm feeds me painkillers, I gather. The injections hurt, leaving a searing sensation in the skin for a few minutes. They asked me to stand up—just once for today. A far worse experience, yet quite manageable. They want me to get better from whatever they have done to me. I felt nauseous, suddenly. Suddenly, I vomited. Just as quickly, the nausea was gone. A purple liquid had come out, dyed by the cranberry juice I had ingested earlier.

I remember now. I asked for this. Yet what a peculiar place, what a peculiar people. Some speak of chop chop—vaginoplasty, one of them said—as a transformative moment. The most life-changing event of all; my life will never be the same. The thought annoys me. I do not wish nor expect to be a whole new person. I cared enough to cheat at the strangers' dehumanizing games and welcome the pain of their scalpels. It is *cool*. Yet, I am no less the same person. My expectations were mundane. To expect is to invite disappointment. Deep in my cynicism, I relish in seeing my altered body as transfiguration—a way of making mine a body I did not recognize, shaping a poetic rhyme out of previously alienating flesh.

The ambient warmth had me bare my right

breast. I proclaimed to everyone who wished to hear me that I did so in emulation of classical paintings. In truth, I could not bare the left one due to the plastic wire in my arm. The strangers seemed amused by my extravagance, enough that they brought in my parents and partner as a gift. These progenitors of mine brought flowers, for which I am so fucking gay. My lover brought a little pink plushie dragon. I chose to cherish them. Liv is their name, and her gender best described as a goddess who wants nothing to do with your puny notions of gender. She and I are one. With a dragon's eye, they watch over me. Protects me with her magic. I enjoyed the company of familiar faces in the strange room. But the drugs made me drowsy, and so I need rest. As I fell asleep, I thought of the fact that despite the pain, it was happiness that brought me closest to tears today.

One of the strangers woke me up after the sun had set to inject more painkillers into me. The pain is manageable, only spiking when I raise my torso. But my butthole, oh lord, it itches. I feel a pressing need to pee, but a bag attached to a tube coming out of me already collects my urine. Phantom penis, stop thinking you need to pee. You do not. You do not even exist anymore. How ignorant of you.

There is a numb sensation spreading in my taint, almost like needing to defecate. My heels hurt from laying down immobile on my back. I complained, and the strangers brought me padding to elevate my feet. Falling asleep, my mouth twitches as if suckling on something. Perhaps it is my body's way of saying I miss penises… in my mouth? Ah, oral fixation, how I have missed you these last twelve hours.

No, seriously, my butthole itches. Unable to sleep, I found my phone on the table next to me and began writing an inane post in the dead of the night. A penis-turned-vagina ought to be named a *pecunt*—pronounced like 'pecan' with a 't,' and a fake British accent.

Day II. The strangers woke me up at the brink of dawn to change my bandages. All but one were immaculate and, even then, 'twas barely a tinge of yellow on the otherwise pristine fabric. Very little did I bleed, the pouch of blood draining my insides having seen but a few drops over the entire night. Without a measure for comparison, my healing strikes me as exceptional thus far. Resting in bed, I spent the early hours thinking about how fascinating it was, observing the strangers work after having read endlessly about their work reconfiguring genitals. To be on this side of the equation, to have my genitals reshaped—it feels a bit surreal. When I woke up, it took me a second to remember the surgery, and yet another to believe it. A heavy weight is lifted from my shoulders, after weeks of freaking out amplified by anxiety. Ceasing medication a few weeks beforehand and living through the onset of hormonal imbalance was hellish. I never expected to feel unambiguously happy as I do. In truth, I expected far more mixed feelings. But no. Then again, I *am* known for having a certain fondness for pain.

Two strangers came to check on me, introducing themselves as surgeons—the butchers. They asked how I felt, and confirmed that their work had been flawless and without complications. I understood their words, but their manner was bizarre— dispensing advice for that which they had never lived. The bruises on my lower abdomen hurt to the touch, though they hurt little. I was denied medication before breakfast, for it would risk nausea. And so, I must wait. The pain is steadily increasing. A little over half an hour to go, and my patience wears thin. They fed me breakfast. It was good. A iögo, some oatmeal, and some cranberry juice— privatized medicine is an injustice. Alas, they made me wait even longer for the painkillers. My comedic side has gone now that I am unmedicated.

One of the strangers made me walk a circle around the large hall. It tugged on one of my stitches, feeling like a weight was pulling downwards inside my vagina. I compared it to a steel ball; someone said cobalt. It may not matter much which metal substantiates the metaphorical ball inside me. After the walk, we refreshed my bandages and the stranger confided in me that, in seven years of work, she had never seen so little bleeding. The bag collecting my urine was tinted by a drop of blood, turning it the shade of a tasty, tasty old-fashioned apple juice. I am thirsty.

For lunch, the food was yet again surprisingly good. I am irked as a hypocritical communist. I share the strange room with another like me. She and her family are kind and funny. Nerdy and punny to exception—just how I like them. The pain is back. The new medication they gave me does not last; I will go back to the old one—Dilaudid, they said. The pain came rushing back when I sat up to eat. Because they already gave me the new drug, I must wait another twenty minutes for the old one. To pass the time, I cuddle my dragon and rabbit plushies. Or is it a hare?

You will be glad to read, dear, that the Dilaudid took effect. I am now well. Enough to take pictures of my bare breasts and trade them to a lovely human on the book of faces. Thanks to my religious qualm with clothing, I have been topless all day.

The strangers probably believe me rather queer, especially as I proclaimed out loud my disdain for clothes and asked them to pass the plastic tube through my gown so as to remove it completely. On every walk, we must redo this dance—I cannot walk naked in the halls. My second stroll of the day was quite hurties. Nonetheless, I circled twice around the room, powering through like a big girl. Are you proud, dear?

I find sorrow in not having a penis anymore, putting me on the regular market instead of being a hot, rare commodity for sugar daddies.

I cannot believe I just had my dick chopped off. The fact of it is so amazing, beautiful, surreal! Sublime, in the romantic sense of the term—it transcends mere mortal affairs, makes them feel so meaningless. As though I am looking down from the tremendous heights of a cliff toward the murderous spikes straddling a stream of water below. Yet it also feels too messy to be sublime, too… human. Is messiness not also sublime? Does humanity not transcend itself?

My urethra is pulsing. My brain locates this sensation to the tip of my penis. A peculiar feeling. I heard a voice through the door saying "that's what she said" in a valley girl accent. I wonder what they were talking about. My genitals hurt. An unpleasant but manageable pain. I have walked three loops around the hall. I hurt less and less with time. The strangers removed the tube from my arm after dinner, which was rather tasty—a chicken wrap with couscous. My flexibility is returning and I can now flex my legs partway in bed. No longer do I have to lay on my back like a plank. God knows I am terrible at being this straight.

Day III. Morpheus must have visited me, for I did not wake in the night; I have little now to report. Can you believe I have a vulva and vagina? I still find it hard to believe, especially since I have yet to see it. The most I saw was the bandage stitched to my skin. Its curve was flat enough to confirm I no longer have a penis—because clearly strangers cannot be so trusted at their word. Imagine if they had colluded to lie about having operated on me. It really would have been the biggest dick move…

Oh shit! I forgot to make a mold of my penis. How will I go fuck myself when people tell me to?!

I wonder if, once I am healed, I will begin having sex with cis men without telling them I am trans. On one hand, it is pretty hard for me to hide the fact, given that it is all I ever talk about. On the other hand, it would make it far easier to have a quick, casual lay.

The stranger forgot I had asked for some relief from pain, making receipt longer than usual. The two who introduced themselves as surgeons returned. In a few hours, I will be heading down the block to a house of some sort, where I will recover for a week. I will be more mobile there and slowly regain bodily function. I wonder if strangers will be there too, and if they will be of a different kind. I cannot wait— being bedridden is killing my legs and back. I have tried resting slightly more on my side to ease the discomfort, but the position hurts and can only be held for so long.

I am thinking about surgery and its meaning. Why would anyone choose me over a cisgender woman? Having now lost the unique shape that was once carved in my loins, am I not but a pastiche, a mediocre forgery of their form? I feel less trans. Maybe even a normie. But then I remember a poem I read last week. Surgery makes me the messy human that I am, and being human is all there is. Remember how I felt the first time I heard The Mountain Goats' *All Hail West Texas*? That's how human I feel. If I am loved, it will be for my messiness.

Oh my god, I have a vulva! That's so wholesome

I want to cry. I cannot wait to see it. The journey to the healing center was arduous, though it is but next door. I am proud of myself for walking up the stairs. I now have my own room, which is lovely. It is huge.

Yikes. After some time in my room, laying on the outsized bed, a stinging sensation engulfed my crotch. I think the sensation of my urethra hurting is, rather, clitoral pain from being cut to measurements. Just before leaving the hospital, the other in my room spoke of how she wanted to shave. I do not believe I brought my razor; perhaps I did not know I would be coming here, or merely forgot. Or did I not want it? That is also possible. The strangers will have to endure my 'fuck the cis' beard. When I moved to the new building, a stranger called me *madame*. I refused, refused to erase my non-binariness and its cosmic horrors. Not today. Not in this sterilized world, where the burden of normative expectations weighs me. I have no wish to be a woman or pretend. I am not—I am a gorgeous biorg witch with flowers in her hair. The metaphor's pronouns are 'she/her,' not mine. I am a glimpse at the essence of the sublime peeped through a keyhole. Gender cannot constrain me; I am Shehulk! Which would explain my inability to put on socks without aid—I must be too ripped.

Holy moly, removing the drain hurts. It did not take long, but the first centimeter the strangers took out was extremely painful—why, it must be punishment. My right leg cramped up, making me wonder if something had gone wrong with the removal. Maybe I am bleeding internally. Or it is just a leg cramp due to, you know, barely moving over the last few days. I am now wearing a pad, which brought about an odd sentiment of validation, although I would probably find it far more validating if the painkillers would *just fucking kick in*. The Mountain Goats are still playing on repeat in my head, rent-free. The toilet welcomed my ass, and I peed without assistance using the valve of the tube coming out of my skin, the catheter. It felt good. Since the bag of urine was removed, I feel like a robot when I pee. *Evacuating waste material, beep boop*, as the pee comes out of the tube upon releasing the latch. Hot damn, I *just* went and already I feel like peeing again. Give or take the dizziness of painkillers, I am mostly back to my normal psychological functioning. Which isn't saying much, I must admit. I cannot wait to see my vulva. Chop chopped, away went the penis! Pebis? Bepis? I already forget how to spell it. Chop me up, Scotty!

Lunch was good—I love a big juicy wiener in my mouth—but sitting at the communal table wasn't exactly painless. I wonder how my brain will remap my junk. Will the tip of my clit feel like the tip of my penis, the brain merely updating its position, or will it create a whole new location-sensation for my clit?

I bet my vagina looks like a gross gaping hole right now.

My farts have turned into cramps. But I doubt I will poop right away, given the medication I've been on… never mind, I pooped. It felt so weird, too! My butthole is sore. The other patients will resent me for pooping so early. They, too, wish to poop. Poop. Poop is such a funny word.

Day IV. One of the people who arrived today at the recovery center is attractive, and I have a mini-crush. I saw her today on a dating app and super-liked her, but she has not liked me back. Oh well. I am eating nerds that my partner brought me last night. Cuddling was fun. I like cuddling. Today was boring. I am sad that I cannot shower until tomorrow—I either counted the dates wrong or the strangers gave me the incorrect date to keep me in a state of bewilderment. The cast-slash-bandage over my crotch is hardening, pulling on the stitching to my pubis. The strangers disallowed me from taking my second Dilaudid for yet another hour, saying I can only complete my dose within the first hour if I choose to take a single tablet. Next time, I will know to ask for two regardless of need. I worry that this will make it harder to discontinue the drug upon leaving. If I ever leave.

The strangers' pleasure seems boundless; my sister visited me. She asked about my vagina, so that was a thing that happened. She drew butterflies on a booklet that the strangers gave me. A sort of healing manual. The entire building seems to be a butterfly museum. The walls are covered with art of the creatures. Later, my progenitors visited again. My mother and I told off my father for not knowing the difference between vulva and vagina—is that what sisterhood feels like? The more the cast hardens, the more I feel like my penis is still there, barely just being grazed by the inner side of the cast. Freaky.

Day V. I did not sleep well last night. The stitching has long begun to pull on my skin, distractingly painfully. The strangers said we would take off the bandages sewn to my cunt later today. My vulva will probably look gross. It'll be *awesome.*

"Good morning ladies," at breakfast. I refuse. At least they always use my name instead of Miss-Last-Name when drugging me, which I appreciate. Having the bandages removed felt so strange— especially when they cut the individual stitches, releasing the taut skin. Far more fear than hurt. Now I must ice my fanny for the quarter of an hour before

showering and finally getting to see my monstrous
vulva. I enjoyed seeing the skin detach from the
bandages and return to its natural position. I was,
however, remonstrated for calling such things cool
and fun. Apparently, mine is an unusually morbid
fascination with messy bodies, one that is not shared.
I have just taken a picture and, sadly, my cunt does
not look nearly as gruesome as I had hoped. My
vulva is swollen—almost swole—but it is far from the
disgusting sight that my ghoulish psyche had hoped
for. The little end of a condom pokes through my
vagina, which I found hilarious—as though I had
sex and just forgot to take it out. To finally shower
was liberating; who knows where the strangers'
hands have been. Weirdly, it did not hurt to touch
my newfound genitalia. At last, I can be my true self:
naked. The strangers ordered it.

I no longer have a penis, though I do have a
peepee—the catheter. It is like a robot penis. I felt a
tinge of sadness looking in the mirror after peeing.
That little dick was cute as heck. Rest in peace, dear.
This whole surgery thing was laborious, all for my
penis to hang out inside. I cannot wait to have sex
with a cishet guy and ask him: "Oh babe, how does
it feel fucking a penis with your penis?"

I napped and woke up to my heels hurting. I am
grumpy. Furthermore, bathing was not as soothing

as showering. My genitals stretching as I sit down caused some pain. I am glad my parents did not visit long. With all their visits, we no longer have much left to tell each other. The stent—that's what the condom is called—is hurting me, pushing to get out and distending the skin, which is ready to rupture. I cannot wait to have it out. But in the meantime, it is making it hard to sleep.

Day VI. O, dear lord, removing the stent felt so weird. It did not hurt but was the most peculiar of feelings—a pulling in my crotch followed by the blissful sensation of freedom. The pogo stick was gigantic. I can't wait to get rammed by a dick of that size—plastic or skin, I am not picky. The happiness awash over me was alas tainted by some overt defense of islamophobia on an online forum I perused, with moderators threatening to ban those who spoke out against it. You cannot ask for liberation while tolerating the same toxic bile directed at others. Of course, you can; we always do. But it should not be so.

As for my vagina, it looks like a gaping hole, and I have nothing to report. Having the stent out brings about mixed feelings; yay I no longer hurt; boo I must now insert hardened dildos in my cunt four times a day and wash *every. single. time.* afterwards. The process eats up half my day. Dilating feels a lot like taking it up the ass, minus the fear of pooping everywhere. I don't dislike it.

Dilating for the second time, I am already tired of it. I just want someone to lock me up in a closet while they make themselves food, before coming back to use me. But no, I have to dildo my life away for the next three months.

Day VII. The strangers removed my catheter. A brief, mild burning sensation—nothing awful. They gave me a plastic thingamabob to pee in, tasking me with recording how much fluid I exude each time. I peed about an hour later. It was hard at first—my shy bladder reflex kicked in—but I eventually succeeded. A lot. Most of it went on my leg and trickled down into the peething, with a bit going in the toilet. I am surprised at how much liquid that was!

The first dilation of the day is terribly unpleasant. Dilating rearranges the muscles. They are inside thinking, like: "Um, what's this? This doesn't belong here. It's in the way." I must train them, as if introducing a new pet to the household. There was almost no blood on the dildos afterward, which is a notable improvement. Chunks of dead skin and blood came out during the vaginal douche, but that is apparently normal and honestly feels good—it makes me feel cleaner, like popping blackheads. *Cleanse the corruption!*

Little pale red hairs adorably poke through the wine-red bruise on my pelvis. I was struck with sorrow just now, seeing myself in the mirror. Not because of any regret or dissatisfaction—fear not. But because I suddenly feel less trans. I know that makes no sense, but it makes me sad because being trans is such a huge part of me and I feel less so, now. What am I, if not trans. I shall have a dick tattooed. And t4t. Trans/gender confirmation tattoos. To resume sitting comfortably without any pain was a source of much enjoyment. I showed my sister a picture of my vulva, and she said it reminded her of Deadpool's face. It feels weird saying 'my vulva'!

I said phantom penis, but it may be less a phantom sensation than a confused sensation. I know which part of the penis the sensation would be in, but not what it corresponds to on my rearranged and stitched-up body. If it feels like my foreskin, is that my clit? My small lips? Is it itching inside my vagina? The excessive swelling of my vulva makes it feel like I have testicles at times.

My partner peed in the measuring cup

thingamabob, out of curiosity. They peed 350 milliliters; I pee anywhere from 450 to 700 milliliters each time. I also made them cum twice, which felt a bit naughty. Dilating again, I realized that being propped up—even slightly—makes the experience far more painful. Tonight went more smoothly; I laid flatter on my back.

I am relaxing in the bath, feeling comfortable. My lover is gone, but I can still feel them here with me, here in spirit. I feel fuzzy inside, like the strangers replaced my stomach with furby fur. Everything is going well. Life is good. I am happy. I haven't felt this good, this relaxed in nigh a month.

Day VIII. One of the others recovering here had her catheter re-inserted for a week. She had been unable to pee due to swelling. My vagina has an unpleasant smell when I clean it, making me feel rather self-conscious. The largest dilator chafed me. The stranger said it was probably from other causes, but I have my doubts for inexpressible reasons. The strangers said I could leave tonight instead of tomorrow morning—I did not know I could leave tomorrow morning. I bid adieu to the strangers; some were kind, all were strange. My parents brought me back to their house. Travel irritated my crotch and made it swell enough that I had to ice it for hours. I punctured the top of a douche with a drill to make sure it spouts to the end of my vagina, to better clean it. I saw myself wearing nothing but panties, which was delicious. But I want to cry from my lack of hips. You win some, you lose some. Time for bed.

The text of which you now hold a transcription was uncovered on a Wednesday morning in the bookshelves of the basement of my childhood house. Unsigned, it appears to recount with no doubt some creativity the narrator's experience in the aftermath of vaginoplasty, in too much detail for it to be apocryphal. Lest readers confuse the writing for my own, I must admit to finding the similarities with my own life uncanny. Not only do I share the author's musical taste but also, to some extent, surgical history and thematic interests. Nevertheless, I do not remember writing it, and so it cannot be mine. Inquiring with my parents, I received only the answer that it had to be. I can only conclude that it came into their hands by magic or coincidence, which are the same.

The authorless writing appears autofictional, using the device of feigned ignorance to cast light onto the process of curiotization undergirding trans medicine. Whereas the trans object is traditionally social curios, the reader is instead interpellated into imagining surgeons and healthcare staff, no doubt some of whom nurses, with the same intrusive gaze. The stumbling stream of consciousness of the disoriented and rather peculiar narrator opens a window into the messiness of bodies and into the queerness of medicine with its arcane rules and suffocating sterility. One is left wondering about a world where medicine, rather than transitude, turns into a spectacle. Perhaps even exoticized; I would be remiss not to remark on the author's copious borrowings from orientalist literature in the vein of André Gide's *L'Immoraliste* or Albert Camus' *L'Étranger*. The allusions to the latter are, if anything, lacking in subtlety. It is unclear if the erotica was intended to be read alongside the surgical experiences; though well-written and thematically harmonious, it is narratively incongruous and utterly superfluous.

The story unfolding through first-person narration resists in plain and subtle language alike the meaning-making of medical power. In the narrator's absurd ignorance, we may read a conscious refusal to stabilize transitude and its attendant desires. Though the device is reminiscent of Samuel Beckett's *Malone meurt*, an impression only heightened by the setting, its wits attempt something of a Borgean air, seemingly in the hopes of subverting the expectations of medical autoethnography. Where the literature would traditionally offer transformative change as an anchor, medicine is displaced, and we are presented with a romance of the mundane; verbiage that connotes the lived life transcendent in its messiness.

Yet as readers, we must ask ourselves whether the author succeeds in their audacious enterprise. Though no doubt well-read the author may be, all the more overburdened and incongruous is their *plume*. The prose is overanxious to astonish and, in the process, finds itself frustrated by the reductiveness of its gimmick. Are we convinced of the narrator's ignorance despite endless contradictions and stylistic blemishes? Let me express my doubts. But if we indeed are, a piece of the puzzle would still be missing—the narrator's ignorance cannot escape, let alone transcend, the definitional role of medical technologies. However much we may be more than our own making, creation remains forever inescapable. The narrator, whoever they may be, forgets a relentless truth. To resist, one must recognize their restraints.

i have a question. should i raise my hand? ugh. speaking up in public is stressful. i don't want to draw attention to myself. i already feel like people look at me weird. plus it's more womanly not to speak up, right? we even measured it last semester. hey, that's totally sexist. isn't that a reason to ask the question, then? i mean… fuck sexism plus it might make other women in the class more comfortable asking and answering questions. ah, what the heck, i'll ask it… interesting. that so doesn't answer my question, though. oh well! …what if people are thinking right now that i am speaking up because i was born with a penis? maybe other women in the class want to speak up even less now because some dude in a dress in monopolizing the space. you're even wearing a dress. oh shut up, brain, you're derailing. at the end of the day, i am a woman and they know it. but do they? what if they only say that to be politically correct but deep down don't see me as a woman? it's not like they can control involuntary impressions. those are the scariest. that sucks. i hate being trans. no i don't. i just hate cissexism. and sexism. hah, i guess that means i hate the world. haha. ha… well, crap. now i feel like shit and i missed, like, half an hour of content. maybe i should just go home. but then people will look at me when i get up. and lay judgy eyes on me. i guess i'll just play with my phone until class is over. yeah, that'll do.

Vaginomancy

I fell face down on the bed, quivering. While I recovered from my orgasm, tremors ran through my body. I could hear them snickering around me, snickering *at* me. Nothing mean, no. They were simply amused by how easy it was, bringing me to climax and leaving me a blubbering mess sprawled on the bedsheets. Later, while chatting, they expressed appreciation for my effortless orgasms. One of them pointed out that they were a useful motivational tool for teaching the other to top. "Instant gratification," he called it.

I, too, find my orgasms absurd lately. Until a few months ago, my 'normal' was for orgasms to be a tedious ordeal. On a good day, I needed at least half an hour to reach them. On worse days, nigh an hour was required—if I could climax at all.

May 22nd was the date of my surgery. Doctors

call it a vaginoplasty, but I call them boring. For four months after vulvaworking, I still couldn't climax, no matter how long or hard I tried. My horniness was debilitating, and the multi-hour magic wand sessions—*please, dear lord, please finally grant me release*—only made me hornier. I was still in the early stages of healing, and masturbation had a masochistic feel to it: I repeated it every few days against my best judgment, knowing it would bring me pain.

Four months on the dot after getting my bespoke vulva, I pushed a finger past the elastic band of my penguin print bottoms while watching television. The pressure of the finger on my clitoris didn't feel much different from the countless previous times, but less than a minute later, my breath held itself. I felt my muscles tighten, pushing out a squirting orgasm. Recovering my wits moments later, I adjourned to the bedroom to confirm replicability. After each orgasm, brought on in a matter of minutes, I desperately tried again, fearing that I was experiencing but a fluke. These repeated orgasms couldn't be permanent, could they?

Months have passed. I am only starting to get used to them. Beyond the thrill of novelty and the sheer ecstasy of *la petite mort*, the upheaval of my orgasmic experiences challenged my sense of erotic self.

Climaxing so readily, I feel like a different person

to my sexual partners and, through them, to myself. Prior to vaginomancy, I took on a subservient role in the bedroom—or wherever else we were having sex. In erotic being-with-others, I sought to pleasure them, most often orally or digitally. I pleased them sexually and found my pleasure bathing in their moans or awaiting the rush of endorphins following the sting of pain. I rarely found enjoyment in having my own erogenous zones stimulated. My pleasure lay primarily in their bodies, not mine. And their pleasure laid in what I did for them.

Now, erotic life has remade its home within my body. When I lie a blubbering mess, shaking on the bed, my pleasure is much too primal to be mediated by others'. They are pleasuring me. We are pleasuring each other. A proximity and reciprocity that used to elude me now structure most of my encounters. I no longer solely find pleasure through them.

The sexual partners from earlier nicknamed me 'Doll,' Before, my nickname would probably have been 'Slut.' Telltale of a shifting portrait of play-acted sexual dynamics, the moniker 'Doll' also speaks of the repurposing of my body as an instrument of pleasure. The doll leads an aesthetic life and is a passive participant in the scene. The slut leads a sensuous life and is an active participant in the scene. The slut is played *with*. The doll is *played* with. The aesthetics of my dollhood, I surmise, are not only predicated by aesthetic attraction, but are also intimately related to my new orgasms. I am not just a beautiful doll. I also produce aesthetic-erotic satisfaction in the way I tremble and flush an exquisite crimson shade when I climax.

For some—not the companions I mentioned, but others—the erotic performance that is my orgasm isn't just a matter of pleasure. It becomes a matter of ego, with my orgasms serving as a measure of their sexual prowess and, often, of their manhood. I was warned this would happen by a partner of mine who climaxes with similar ease. They told me of the men who saw our orgasms as little more than ego boosts to collect as though their virtues as lovers had anything to do with the rapidity of our O's. Look, *dude*, the sight of a well-curved piece of wood would probably do the trick. You're not that special. These are, of course, never the sexual partners who would think to suggest orgasm denial as an addition to our repertoire. They measure pleasure by my orgasms, not the satisfaction of my desires.

My phenomenological shift from erotic sluthood to erotic dollhood isn't solely attributable to pussycrafting. My recent sexual trauma has also made me crave caring dynamics, which translates into a less active role on my part. Being more passive compels partners to confirm their attentiveness to my needs and desires, and their attentiveness heals me.

This sexual trauma cannot be divorced from my newfound yonic form, either. I found myself in a vulnerable situation because I was eager to try out my new vagina, and I ended up hurt. And that trauma can't erase the role that new sensations played in reconfiguring my sexual identity—one could even say personal identity, given how leading a role sexuality plays in my life. When and how my sense of self will stabilize remains to be seen. Let us together pray that I won't become a pillow princess. A princess *simpliciter* seems preferable.

Never have I ever had to warn people I might cum from kissing before. That it was a realistic possibility had eluded me when she and I were on the couch at my apartment, chatting. I was consumed by apprehension, awaiting her response to my question: would you like to kiss? I later learned she was even more apprehensive than I was. It had been years since she had last been with a woman.

We made out, lying sideways on the lounging couch, hesitant to embrace fully. Her lips were plumper than mine and shifted around agreeably, leaving me enough time to gently bite and pull on her lower lip, relishing in its texture. Her tongue was pleasantly tasteless, leaving behind but a faint reminiscence of the tea we had drunk earlier.

I started shaking, overcome by an orgasm. A small one, sure, but any orgasm is probably noticeable enough to warrant an explanation in this context.

Embarrassed, I explained that I climaxed comically easily nowadays and hoped that it didn't make her uncomfortable. She said it didn't. She seemed mildly entertained, if anything. We resumed kissing, and I had a sprinkling more spontaneous *oh*~'s before she returned home.

That initial orgasm left a nagging feeling of guilt in its wake, though. It had made the situation more sexual than either of us intended at that point. Our sexual interaction was no longer about two mouths, but now also included my vulva—even though we were still too shy to pet each other's curves.

Beyond the discomfort I felt from imposing on her a sexual overtone that we had not previously discussed, my climax also left me feeling alienated from my body. It had done things contrary to my intention and without my knowledge. It's one thing to climax from slow humping, but how can I feel at home in my body and sexuality when the mere sight of an attractive couple in a TV series—Cisco and Cynthia, for those who may be wondering—is enough to make me cum?

I also came, with someone else, when penetration was hurting me; when I later described what happened as sexual abuse. I came, even though I didn't like it. Both my experience with sexual violence and with my spontaneous orgasms reveal a distance and disconnect between my body and I, a distance and disconnect which was heretofore hidden by the sheer persistence and conscious effort required to orgasm. I couldn't cum without wanting to. Now I can.

Embodiment is often assumed to be a consensual experience. Reflexive, involuntary, and spontaneous actions are known to occur, but they're largely absent from prevailing narratives of agency. They're treated as exceptions we need not concern ourselves with, doubtless because acknowledging the occasional command of body over mind would undermine the ableist Enlightenment models of rationality that underpin neoliberal social orders.

Bodies are widely understood as tools set to our own purposes. But now, I apprehend my body less as a tool than as a companion, our relationship wandering between consensual, antagonistic, and unexpected.

I let out a moan. His cock was pleasant inside me, rhythmically beating against my prostate. A thought traversed my mind, and I began giggling, hiding my mouth behind my hands so as to feign innocence and cutesy. I asked him: "Oh yeah, babe, how does it feel fucking a penis with your penis?"

Suppressing a chuckle, he responded in a playful tone: "So good. How does it feel having your penis fucked by a penis? Don't you love it when I fuck your inverted penis?" We burst out laughing, unable to keep our queer faces straight any longer. A few moments later, I came, and we turned our attention back to fucking, closing out the amusing chapter.

One of my fears with cuntsmithing was that it would undo the queerness of my body. Nagging at the back of my mind was the thought that having a penis made me *more* trans, *more* special, *less* of a normie. Because if I lose my transitude, what do I have left? How would I fill the void left behind as the transitude oozed out of me by the pussy?

In her work on grotesque bodies, Sara Cohen Shabot highlighted how the figure of the cyborg, which rose to prominence through the work of Donna Haraway, risks being idealized and turned into a normative, hyper-gendered figure. If there was ever doubt in my mind that this could happen, T-800 and T-X from the Terminator franchise put the final nail in my cyborg dream's coffin. But that's okay, because I prefer Shabot's figure of the grotesque, anyway.

Frankenstein's monster—a trans lesbian if I ever saw any—reminds me of the figure of the grotesque. A treasured character in the trans imaginary ever since Susan Stryker penned *My Words to Victor Frankenstein Above the Village of Chamounix: Performing Transgender Rage*, the stitched-up monster, the biorg, shares much in common with grotesque creatures. Surgically constructed yet exceeding the will of its maker, the biorg challenges the separation between self and world. In the words of Shabot, "we are *in* the world and our bodies are open to it and to others, but our boundaries are nebulous."

A biorg, I am in excess of the surgical moments that shaped my body. My monstrous agency, the one which makes me human, allows me to redefine vaginomancy—a surgery often depicted as normalizing—as a queer event. My vagina affectionately becomes an inverted penis, an innie, a frankenpussy, in my mouth.

Is Frankenstein's monster conforming
to society
for not being a mound of rotting flesh?

I will always be sewn together,
flesh-bound to be as grotesque
as I am sublime
the essence of my humanity
expressed in the messiness of my body

Constituting myself in these terms is not as unchallenging as my words may suggest. The curse of biorgs is that, though students of excess, we remain stitched-up from parts originating in others. Our bodies always carry the meanings that were bestowed by these others, and resisting, moving beyond these meanings is an arduous task. I aspire to construct my body as queer, but some days I do wonder if I ever will succeed. I am afraid I might not.

I like to say that I picked the alien model before hitting the 'craft' button. Vulvas show an astonishing range of appearances, including bespoke vulvas. Mine looks unlike any I have seen, though, even compared to those fashioned by the same surgeon.

Proclaiming my pussy looks weird, alien-like inevitably invites denial and reassurance from well-meaning friends, as though the peculiar, the queer, is undesirable. Yes, I do have mixed feelings about my alien vulva. So many days I wish it simply looked like any of my friends' vintage vaginas—is vintage an appropriate counterpart to bespoke, or are they best called ready-to-eat? Anyway, just as many days I instead relish in taking on an inhuman form, a shape of undeniable queerness, a shape which suits me well, even though I never had predicted it.

Times were dire. I prayed not to lose my capacity to orgasm from the vaginomancy. Religiously, I set up an altar on my bed, sacrificing daily my virginal self in an hour-long ritual involving a wand.

Prayed, because I didn't know if I would ever be able to climax again, despairing at the days passing by, bringing me closer and closer to four months post-chop chop without a single orgasm. My fear was perhaps disproportionate given the clitoral sensations I quickly regained, but the future nevertheless seemed wide open. Had I not heard of fellow transfems losing their orgasms indefinitely?

Healing was a trial of the unexpected. As much as I assiduously read the words of friends and strangers, their experiences varied wildly, and I now realize how dissimilar the future I imagined was from eventual reality.

Pessimism played a role in my mistaken predictions. I was apprehensive about the possibility of disappointment, so I taught myself to prepare for the worst. But there was also something more to my surprise than just pessimism. I never expected that my body could change me this way. For all the lip service I pay to relational ontology and phenomenology, the changes I underwent were of a kind I altogether failed to predict.

Naively, perhaps, I assumed that my orgasms would only minorly change. I reasoned that hormones were the primary determinants of orgasmic sensation and that surgery would mostly make orgasms easier to attain because of increased comfort in my own body as well as readier access to my prostate—a dynamic which could have been partly mitigated by the trimming of the head of my penis when making the smaller clitoris. I didn't expect a radical shift in how I experienced my body as a locus of erotic life.

The unpredictable forms part and parcel of the gorgeous messiness of humanity. Going under the scalpel was a leap of faith. Looking back, I had no idea what things would be like afterwards, beyond the superficial. Yes, I would have a vulva and a vagina, and yes, I would be happy with them, but what would it *mean* to me, *for* me, to have them?

I am only beginning to figure out answers to these

questions. It has so far meant remaking my erotic relationship to others, reshaping my appreciation of consent and understanding of the consensuality of embodiment, reconstituting the queerness of my body, and embracing the integral openness of the future. Experiences will continue to shape me. I am excited to see how.

Pressing two fingers against the sides of my clitoris, I can feel warmth pulse in and out of my chest like little tingling waves washing onto a familiar shore after a storm. I don't know what the future reserves for me, but this is alright.

aligned now   the line
                    of my crotch
a few notches added   dug
                    in my skin
        marks of another's territory

laying naked in bed my body is alien

   to kiss, feel, lick, enjoy
    it knows to bring to ecstasy
  but the pleasure that's mine tarries

Permission to Hurt

We hadn't exchanged more than a few words before I could feel her pulsating against my tongue as my saliva dripped down her dick. Moaning, she pushed my head down on her shaft. I gagged. She knew I liked the rush of endorphins and adrenalin from restricted airflow, that I delighted in the entrancing panic of being unable to breathe for a few seconds. Up for air, I found myself panting, caught between the ecstatic rush of oxygen and the trepidation of being mere moments from losing it once again.

I must have uttered a few words through the haze because I suddenly found myself on my back as she perched over me, squirting lube on the condom that was now on her cock. I was beyond excited. It would be my first time with a flesh penis inside my bespoke pussy. As she rubbed herself above me, my legs around hers, I told her to be careful and go slow—my vagina was still healing. She inserted herself inside me, her blue eyes locked onto mine as she let out a gasp of pleasure. My eyes rolled back as she pressed herself past my prostate, the slight pain enhancing the overwhelming sensations inside me. I grabbed her thighs, pausing her rocking hips to let my internal muscles accommodate the insertion. Gently thrusting to keep herself hard, I could feel her breasts grazing right above my pelvis as her breath on my open neck contrasted with the cold air of my bedroom. As I eased my hands' pressure on her legs, she caught onto my signal and let our rhythm naturally crescendo.

Alerted by my moans, she brought her left hand to my face and let her thumb trail down my partially opened mouth onto my neck before pressing her thumb and middle finger against my carotids. Gazing upon my lip bite, she pressed harder and harder until my vision began blurring and ants started running across my fingertips. I touched her arm, signaling for her to unclench her fingers to my relieved sigh. Letting go of my neck, she redirected her grasp to my right thigh, etching a plum and juniper hematoma into my skin as a memento of our encounter.

Her eyes closed to bask in the sensation of my movement up and down her shaft. I asked her to slap me. She pretended not to hear, making me beg. I complied. She whacked me across the cheek, which rosied under her touch. I winced as she lifted her hand again. Concerned, she asked if her strike had been too hard. I appeased her worries, enjoying the instinctual flinching her hand incited as I zoned out of my body and watched from afar in subspace. Carried away, she quickened her rhythm in and out of me, thrusting deeper and deeper. I let out a sudden cry of pain. She gazed at me in horror and jumped back on the bed, revealing bright droplets of blood on the condom. Her voice trembled as she asked me if I was okay. I giggled at her tender attention and reassured her—it happens. I hadn't yet fully healed and small amounts of blood were routine.

So as not to aggravate my vaginal lining, she climbed atop me, throwing the condom wrapped in a tissue onto the empty side of the bed. Obeying her command, I took her in my hand and began masturbating her, sliding my hand in pace with her breathing. Her breaths quickened and intermixed with moans until she orgasmed, leaving a few drops of translucent liquid on my breast. I picked it up with my finger, brought it to my tongue, and pulled her in for a kiss, letting her taste herself. Respectively exhausted by her orgasm and my foray into subspace, we collapsed in each other's arms. I woke up sometime later to the sounds of her picking up her clothing from the floor.

My feelings disorient me. However I reimagine what happened, I cannot erase that feeling of responsibility. Responsibility for not stopping her when she neglected and exceeded my boundaries. I could have said no. After she held me down and I choked up tears on her body, after I felt the panic of my consciousness slipping away, after she ignored my hands pushing back against her hips and my whimpering discomfort—I could have said no. Had I communicated clearly, she may have stopped—did she not ungrasp my neck when I touched her arm? And yet I feel harmed, wronged, hurt. I consented, but not to this. Not this hard. Not bleeding for weeks. Not verging on falling unconscious. Not suffocating on your fucking dick.

Awash in the chemicals caused by pain, fear, and blood rushing to my ears, it becomes difficult to assert myself. That dissociative-like state I know as subspace interferes with my ability to realize my desires. I know that kink communities convene scene negotiations, recognizing the diminished capacity to consent brought on by altered awareness. Renegotiations are often shunned. Ambushed consent—the springing up new activities on those who, inhabiting subspace, are unable to reflect on and affirm their wants and needs—is assault. And if not assault, failing to give competent uptake of submissive partners' imperfect communications of their desires, discomforts, and boundaries remains violative.

Well though I may know these things, I cannot but wonder if my pain is allowable. It was long before I recognized its presence in me. It took me time to realize that my flashbacks were trauma surfaced. Twice I spoke to her before I acknowledged the panic that overtook me each time I saw her on social media and finally blocked her. She may not know the hurt she has caused me. I know she was confused when I unfriended her. Though in my abstract thoughts I appreciate my pain as valid, can I welcome that knowledge in my gut? As I write these words, a stream of questions press themselves into my mind. Is it not mere bad sex, my writing diluting and offending the very idea of sexual violence? Does my hurt even register on the scale of human suffering, compared to what others have lived? Had I not outwardly consented and, at the very least, let her go on without a word? Is it not my fault for surrendering the opportunity to say no? As much as they may try, these preposterous questions cannot erase the feeling that I was wronged.

The chaotic tugging of emotions alit in me, torturing me, diminishing me, I cannot untangle it from the trauma. These doubts in my own moral compass are integral to my pain. I disbelieve my memories. I distrust my sensorial, cognitive, and moral faculties—the very faculties I depend on to flourish. I fear using the term but find myself needing it, if only to end the constant self-torment with a name: sexual abuse. But where does that name leave me? I cannot say, though I worry that it fails to capture the internal turmoil that pains me almost more than the violations themselves. My brain, wherefore art thou gaslighting me?

I began attending therapy again. Not enough, not enough, but I do go. Maybe it will ease the pain. Or maybe it will only bring the emotions to the surface and see my façade of functioning crumple under the weight. Right before we had sex for the first time, a new partner asked me if I would be able to affirm my wants and limits during intimacy. Overcome with the lingering stress of my boundaries being violated, I wept at her question.

Writing these words, there is a sting of shame in my stomach. The memory of my abuse excites me. Maybe it is understandable. Had these acts occurred under an atmosphere of care, with careful consent and preparation, I may have enjoyed them. I long longed for rough sex and degradation, thrived on choking and consensual non-consent, relished in the marks left on my body. Thoughts of such things excite me. Erotic vignettes are only ever a consent away from being sexual violence, and vice versa. Yet, though it makes sense, it makes none. How could I eroticize memories that leave me panicked when they appear as flashbacks? I am left wondering if I do so because of my existing kinky propensities—combined with the abstraction of memories, far less real than flashbacks as they are—or because arousal can serve as a defense mechanism, an unconscious attempt to protect myself from trauma and perhaps even heal. Eros has not stopped the flashbacks, the dissociation, nor the discomfort that takes home at the pit of my stomach. It has not prevented the fight-or-flight response from taking over me when a hand dares approach my neck, even when I know it is not headed for my throat, even when I know that my dear friend would never choke me without first seeking permission.

I rewrote my story to heal. In it I weaved other memories. I changed her eyes. Made her kind. Injected consent and caring attention in the tale. I rewrote my story because I could no longer eroticize an unaltered recollection of my own trauma without embedding it deeper in my psyche. How messed up is it, being aroused at someone abusing you, traumatizing you, depriving you of your sense of self and control?

Ever since it all happened, I struggle to find pleasure in kink. Strides were made recently when I let someone spank me, inscribing a curative pink on my cheeks. A struggle—because kink has long been integral to my self-conception. I'm that kinky slut, yes, it is I, that kinky slut. Or at least I was. Reconfiguring my relation to sex entails rethinking who I am, how I stand in the world. In recent years, I have found myself yearning for softness, as if a caring touch could erase its opposite. Softness is no antithesis of kink, but it is a form that feels foreign to me. And I feel lost.

you said "im sorry"
and you made me cry
as though you gave me permission
to hurt
to cry

and I felt grateful

they call it closure
how does it feel, being grateful
for the wrong people
what does it feel like when you want
need permission

from the wrong people

you're the reason I couldn't cry
couldn't admit my hurt
weren't you?

and now I have tears again because of you
I ache, I hurt
another time because of you

so why the fuck do I feel grateful?

Transcribing my words from an earlier version, I re-identified her gender. She... In its original form, my writing was inflexed with neutrality in a deliberate attempt to hide the gender of the person I spoke of. I feared revealing that I spoke of a trans woman, that I was hurt by someone in the community I breathe and live with. We live in a society so eager to exile trans women at any slight, a world that associates transfeminine bodies with masculinity, with penetration, with danger, with rape. These terms for our bodies are symbolically interchangeable; violence is not what transfeminine bodies do—it is what they *are*. Navigating life knowing that the shape of my body is apprehended as predatory has been deeply traumatic. More so than even the sexual trauma I hold. Little pleases people more than turning trans women into the worst of men, into perpetrators of sexual violence. Worse—a thousand times worse—if she has a penis. Worse—a million times worse—if she is sexually dominant. Yet nothing in what I experienced distinguished her from the violence perpetrated by cisgender women, which are as common as they are discounted. She has a penis, of course, but my hurt could not care less; it is the violation that pains, not the dick.

Nothing distinctly gendered in my tale but for the fear that taints the retelling of my experience— knowing transmisogynistic venom can all-too-easily be crafted from it. Long I refused to imagine how my words would be distorted into a weapon in a world that does not need sexual violence to turn trans women into patriarchal invaders.My silence was a refusal to be instrumentalized by those who hunger for the demonization of transfeminine bodies. Your circles—our circles—were never immunized against these reactions. There are myriads of allegorical anti-vaxxers in our midst. No barriers to transmisogyny were ever erected in our streets. For the transmisogyny that pervades us, carrying the pernicious lie that penises are tantamount to masculinity and rape, we are rewarded with silence. I have no doubt that many before me have silenced the gender of those who hurt them out of fear that speaking would facilitate discursive and material violence against transfeminine people. So, too, will many after me.

Silence erased me. Without naming her gender, I cannot expose the betrayal and psychic conflict that raged in me. I trusted her not just because she spoke gently, but because I saw myself in her. She was my kin, my family. I needed to be able to trust her, and yet she betrayed me none the less. And when I needed to speak my hurt, the words refused themselves out of my mouth. It would have been easier had she not been trans. Can healing proceed in silence? In the opportunity of confronting transmisogyny, I found an aperture through which to name her as a trans woman. I speak so those who carry t4t and sapphic trauma etched into their skin may feel heard. As for her identity, I doubt I will ever reveal it. Scratch that—I never will. I have neither the strength nor the weakness to see her ostracized, to risk her blood on my hands. Social death is often literal death, to trans women.

Since I began drafting this chapter, she spoke to me. The prospect of her ignorance angered me— how dare she, *how fucking dare she* lay unaffected while I tortured myself? Unblocking her, I spat at the harm she caused me. Her first reply was: "I'm sorry." I broke down crying. So sorry to have hurt me. Months of bottled-up tears cascaded down my cheeks. It wasn't her intention. She regretted it. The pressure in my sinuses subsided, as though I needed her permission to hurt. To heal.

She told me she stopped sleeping around upon realizing the pain she caused me. Maybe she speaks the truth. Maybe she did initiate the process of introspection necessary to protect others. We did not speak since. I cannot tell if her disregard for my boundaries was callous or careless. A bad submissive may be boring, but a bad domme is traumatizing. Months after speaking, a mutual acquaintance messaged me to ask if what she had told them was true. Disinterested in revisiting my pain to satisfy the curiosity of a stranger with obscure motives, a stranger who showed themselves at best insensitive to my needs, I told them to fuck right off. However inopportune, the question seems to confirm that she takes responsibility for what she did to me.

Neither demon nor monster, she who hurt me is human. Human, with all that comes with it. Fear, pain, errors. She hurt me. She harmed me. I will always be healing from her. But beyond hurt, I also hold hope. I am not religious, but I believe in redemption.

it hurts
        it feels good but it hurts
    her breasts grazing my pubis
        as she slides in too deep
    I fear I might be bleeding
how long will it hurt?
        am I broken?
            do I regret this?   will I?
    will my body ever feel mine?

i'm moaning
        it feels good
                but I can barely feel anything
a pinch of pain
    a haze of pleasure so slippery I wonder if it's
    really there

and her weight atop me
    we kiss
    her eyes are blue and reassuring
        with the feet of a smile

                this moment feels

The Men in My Bed

Sitting on the sofa, I can feel his beard pricking my chin while he kisses me. His breath smells of the dumplings we had for lunch down the street, before I invited him back to my apartment. Not quite a turn-on. As he timidly fondles my breast through my dress, I slowly lay my hand on his crotch and, gauging his reaction by a moan, begin massaging him through the jeans. Soon, I began tugging at his waistband, inviting him to pull it down. Am I enjoying this? Am I into him? My meager attraction hangs on but he's nice enough; I've been enjoying our chat. His attraction to me is conspicuous and being wanted turns me on. Having sex is just easy.

Noticing my hand at his waist, he pauses and extends himself, pulling out a wallet from his tauntingly large pocket. It's one of those ugly black leather wallets, the same my dad owns—old with a spreading white scar across the face. Fumbling from nervousness, he pulls out one of those tiny plastic bags I used to carry weed in during my youth. I can see a couple blue pills at the bottom. Reaching for his water on the windowsill, he throws back his head and washes one of the pills down with a gulp. He haphazardly sets the glass back on the edge of the shelf and redirects his attention to me. His hand grazes my nipple as he finds his way back, half-straddling my legs as his other hand slowly pulls my dress up.

Scrolling through my Tinder messages, I was surprised by the number of men in my inbox. I first came out as pansexual when I was about seventeen but, at the time, I would have professed a preference for women over men. Seeing my sexual record before my eyes gave me pause. It's almost all men. I've sometimes heard people say that transitioning changed their sexual orientation. Mine hasn't, in a way—the labels I use have remained constant over the years. Yet everything else feels changed. Having lived as a trans woman for years before asserting a non-binary identity, I have seen the same relationships go from being read as opposite-sex to same-sex to… *insert confused stare*. Nor is it merely a matter of outside perception—my behavior has changed, too. As long as I may have been attracted to men, I haven't always been as comfortable engaging them sexually as I am now. Therein lies a key reason for why my Tinder is so... unseemly male.

There's this misconception, even among queer communities, that embracing your sexuality is a process with a well-defined end. But in my experience, sexual orientations are complicated, especially when intersecting with evolving gender identities. Living in community with queer and trans people has taught me the same—sexuality and gender cannot always fit into easy categories. For those who, like me, struggle with crafting a sense of themselves in the world, acknowledging the inescapable messiness of queer life can be liberating. Demanding order and discipline is for cops, and we don't like cops.

I first called myself pansexual at seventeen, as I began to realize that my longstanding sexual curiosity about men betrayed deeper feelings. Feelings of being pulled toward their mouths for me to kiss— they could not be mere vertigo, mere call of the void. I long resented my parents for their dismissiveness when I told them I was pansexual but, to be honest, the first to disbelieve me was myself. Having only had relationships with girls until that point made me feel insecure in my attraction to boys. And I was hesitant to pursue them due to the expectations I had internalized about gay sex. If I am not a top and am not interested in being on the receiving end of anal sex, could I really be queer? It took me years to shed those sexual scripts associating gay sex with anal sex, years to acknowledge that sex with men could mean whatever the heck I wanted it to mean. Dating men became easier. I had my first sexual experience with a man at twenty-three.

But just as this new world of dating opened itself up before me, I closed the door by transitioning. Transitioning was undoubtedly a positive moment in my life. It changed its course, infused it with *joie de vivre*. Yet I enjoyed the world of queer male dating, and on lonely days I wish it could still be mine. Early in my transition, dating men was difficult. I feared them because they were the ones yelling at me threateningly on the street and throwing stuff my way. Talking to straight men on dating apps was disheartening, weighed by the sheer transmisogyny and fragile masculinity that coated their messages. I simply couldn't expend my energies comforting men in their sexuality when I was at my most vulnerable, naked in their arms. Nor did I have the emotional resilience to wade through hundreds of men to find the one who didn't fear that his attraction to me made him gay, who didn't treat me like a shameful fetish, a warmer sex doll. As for the queer men I met, amazing as some were, I couldn't silence this constant nagging question at the back of my mind, asking me if they were only into me because they liked men.

Things have changed since. Some years ago, I underwent the intricate satanic ritual known as vaginomancy and, tbh, going from a penis to a vulva and vagina has certainly simplified my sex life. While I still sleep with women and non-binary people a fair lot, it is difficult to deny that I sleep with men much more than I used to. No, not because I am more attracted to men but, rather, because sleeping with them is easier. *They* are easy. They are easy, and I have less to fear; their masculine insecurities vanished along with my penis. Their fears of being gay dissipated even though I am non-binary and, thus, less a woman than I once was. I joke that, being gaygender, all attraction to me is by definition *kinda gay*. Discounting my identity, they are nonplussed by my antics. I continue to experience my fair share of transphobia, in part because I refuse to reveal the shape of my genitals on dating apps, but I am no longer as fearful of men's violence. Now hosted in a body that does not challenge their self-conception, all they want is for me to suck their dick on a moment's notice.

My sexploits exceed the male gaze. Sex became easier. Intercourse can now follow a familiar script:

oral, then penetration, then goodbye. Though I am resentful of the existence of these fixed scenarios in the first place, it is hard for me not to be grateful for the ways in which they facilitate my life. Instead of having to navigate and negotiate potentially conflicting sexual interests, I can lie back and let the script work in my favor. In an ironic twist, the things I had to struggle against and deconstruct in my youth are now facilitating my sex life.

Does my increased comfort and sexual intimacy with men translate into a change in sexual orientation? Perhaps. Or not. It depends on how we understand sexual orientation. On the one hand, can we say that sleeping with more men because men are increasingly interested in me constitutes a phenomenological shift? Many cisgender bisexual women date men, not because they are more attracted to them but because they constitute a significantly larger dating pool— and are no less bisexual for it. Nor are they any less bisexual for being terrified of talking to women because, *gosh, girls, pretty~*. On the other hand, my growing comfort with men translates into greater pleasure having sex with them. Although I may feel the same toward them on an erotic-aesthetic level as I did in my teenage years, I cannot deny that I sexually desire them more.

Reflecting on the complexity of queerness, maybe

we should better distinguish sexual comfort, sexual behavior, and sexual identity. Often, they fall out of line with one another. If sexual identity is built upon a deeper sense of self, sexual comfort is often bound up with past traumatic experience, and sexual behavior is dictated in part by who is interested in having sex with you. Not to be trite, but all of that's okay. It's perfectly fine. Some can fit themselves neatly into boxes, but not all can. Learning to find comfort in the messiness of human experience is a queer virtue. Rejecting the call to provide tidy narratives of sexual orientation can be an integral part of queer liberation.

I pull down his foreskin, his penis flaccid in my mouth. As I suck, it hardens and grows between my lips. A moan escapes me as I feel my pussy throb against his knee. His cock half-erect, I pull a condom from the bedside table and straddle him. Sitting atop him, I guide his head to the entrance of my pussy and slowly lower myself onto him.

one drop

two drops

the blood of my arm, dripping on the floor

a ritual of blood and candles and incense

to synthesize death

process violence

the moment her last breath fled her lungs

Triton and the Nereid

"Hey, sexy!" He propped himself up on the rock next to me. I looked up from painting my nails, blushing at the little pet names he gave me, and smiled.

"That's a pretty color! Really works with your tail." I inherited my mom's fiery red hair and emerald tail, whereas he was rocking curly blonde hair against his sparkling golden tail. The water pearling off his abs, aglow in the reflection from his tail, reminded me of Zeus and made me feel a distinctive tingle in my clit. Thank god for fast-drying top coat because I don't know how long I'd've managed to keep my hands to myself.

"How did you sleep?"

"I slept well, you?"

"Fine. Dream of me?"

Well, I won't lie, I wish I had... "No, I didn't."

"That's too bad. What a waste of a good night's sleep."

"Pffft. Conceited much?" I scoffed.

"Just realistic." He grinned. Fucker. He knows very well how hot I find him, and how wild he's been making me ever since we kissed at the dinner party a couple days ago.

"Maybe I dreamed of someone else. Have you thought of that?"

"That possibility escaped my mind. I sometimes forget other people exist when I'm with you..."

Bluuuush. I know he's just flirting but damn. I let out a theatrical gasp, making him giggle.

"Here, let me help." He began blowing on my nails.

Smiling, I slowly brought my hand up to our faces' level, so that he was blowing directly toward my face. I looked at him with my 'kiss me' eyes, blinking very slowly.

"You know, if you're so good at blowing..." I bit my lip and glanced down.

"Hah. So that's how it is, eh? Zero to a hundred

just like that? Where's the subtlety." He grinned.

"Yeah right, like you're Mr. Subtle yourself, with your sex dream allusions. Just, like, okay?"

"I'll have you know I am the essence of subtlety incarnate."

"Like that kiss the other day? Subtle. Oh, and how about yesterday's?"

"Talking about kisses…" He leaned over and kissed me. His lips tasted like seawater. I put my arms around his neck, periodically parting my lips to let his tongue into my mouth. He liked to bite my lower lip, which made me whimper, my hips rocking underneath kisses that made me hornier and hornier.

I ran my fingers through his short hair as his hands held my lower back, slowly yet obviously moving toward my ass. We paused for a moment, holding our heads against each other's, my fingers still tangled in his hair.

He began kissing a line from my cheek to the nook of my neck, which he bit gently, drawing yet another moan out of me and making my hips push even harder against his tail.

"May I?" His left hand gestured toward my bikini top. I nodded enthusiastically.

After a few teasing grabs on the outside of my top, he slid his hand underneath, finding my nipple and taking it between his thumb and index finger.

"Piercing, eh? Fuck, girl, you are so hot." He let out a gasp, signifying his arousal. Seeing him struggle to comfortably massage my nipple from that angle, I unhooked my bikini, giving him plenty of leeway to continue exploring my breasts.

"Do you maybe want to use your mouth?"

"May I?"

"Yes." I moaned as he rested his tongue against my left nipple and began sucking. I took his free hand and motioned downward. Taking the cue, he began petting my tail belt, right over my vulva. Though the scales were thick, I could feel the vibration through to my clit. I was so aroused.

"Would you like me to use my mouth… somewhere else?"

"What did you have in mind?"

"I could go down on you… if you ask nicely."

"You're a fucking genius, Alex." I propped myself up on my elbows to pull down the top part of my tail, revealing my vulva crowned by a trimmed yet visibly fiery red pubis.

"I know." Always cocky, even during sex.

He kissed down my belly before settling in to kiss and gently nibble around my vulva, teasing, never more than brushing against my clit.

"Alex…" Responding to my plea, he put his mouth over my clit and began sucking and licking. The sight of the ocean behind him, with the sun reflecting off both his tail and the water, encircling his gorgeous face so happily eating me out, was stunning. I came nearly instantly and came again and again over the next few minutes.

"Do you want to finger me?" He nodded, slowly inserting a finger into my wet pussy, his lips still around my clit as his tongue ran circles around it.

"Oh fuck, babe. I'm gonna cum. Fuck, fuck, fuck!" I climaxed, squirting all over his face, my whole body shaking.

He came up back to my level and kissed me. I could taste myself on his lips. God, I love the taste of pussy. We cuddled and kissed.

"Is there anything I can do for you?"

"Mmhm, well, I don't like getting fingered, but I wouldn't say no to having my dickclit sucked…"

"Yes, daddy!" I grinned teasingly.

He let out a gasp, almost a moan. I think he liked being called that. He pulled down his own tail, lying down in the sand, his arms behind his head.

Impatient, I took his dickclit in my mouth. Fuck teasing, I needed him *now*. I began sucking him off, assisting with my tongue for added sensation. I held his hips with one hand and laid my other hand on his abs for stability and, well, abs are hot okay?

He tasted amazing and smelled of musk and sea. So arousing. His moans were adorable. The whole scene was so warm and sexy that I spontaneously climaxed while going down on him.

His hips were rocking faster and faster. He put his left hand on my head, aiding my back-and-forth until he suddenly stopped, orgasming. I felt his dickclit pulsate and harden in my mouth. I gave it a few more kisses for good measure before going back up to kiss him, laying in his arms.

"Thanks for that. You're quite good at this…"

"Any time… daddy."

"It's so hot when you call me that." He smiled.

"I somehow seem to have noticed that. I'm glad you liked it."

"You know, I have a really nice strap-on back at

home if you ever want to try it…"

"That sounds like fun… Maybe tonight?"

We cuddled on the sand, enjoying the midday sun reflecting off the water and our tails, warming our entangled bodies.

"Are you hungry? I could go for some anemones right now."

"Sound great! Let's go get some?"

"Yeah, let's go. After you, Ashley."

Sometimes I just want to see myself in the world. An image without fetish, without othering. Mundane, banal. Sometimes, wishing I were just… there.

Libidinal Vertigo

No sooner had I invited her in than I found myself back pinned against the heavy wooden door. The grain pressed into my bare upper back. Her fingertips teased my pierced nipple through my tank top as she licked my neck just below the earlobe. Grazing my skin with her teeth, I felt a chill spread outward from her mouth, like a balloon of fairy dust popped near my carotid. As suddenly as she had come in, she pulled her head back, one hand still on my hip, and asked to shower. She had a client to see later; we only had an hour or so.

I hip-checked the misaligned door to lock it and led her to the bathroom. Periodically checking the temperature of the water against the back of my hand, I gazed at the beautiful creature undressing before my eyes. A tall ginger with flowing hair, she reminded me of her gracious highness Sophie-Anne

Leclerq, *feu* Vampire Queen of Louisiana. Minus the French, of course—that one's mine.

Steered by my hand, she stepped into the bathtub. Her hair darkened to cinnamon in the water. Turning to face me, she beckoned with her outstretched finger—slowly, suggestively. I felt my pussy throb and a clumsy heat disperse across my chest. I pushed the curtains aside and stepped into the bath. As my foot steadied on the wet surface, her hand turned downwards, directing me to my knees. Thanking the gods for hearing my pleas, I obediently kneeled before her, guiding her partly erect cock into my mouth. I closed my eyes, half to escape the drops of water streaming down into them, half to concentrate on overcoming my gag reflex. Her hands guided my head as she tenderly petted my hair and kept it out of my way. Enthusiastically, I began swaying deeper and deeper, soon fitting the entirety of her cock in my throat. I could tell apart the saliva from the running water as it trickled down my chin—stickier, more viscous. Suppressed moans exited through my nose and escaped through gaps in the seal of my throat.

"Come up, little pet," she ordered in a tone that did not admit disagreement. I hoisted myself to her level with the help of her hands pulling beneath my shoulders. The pressure lifted from my knees, I noticed grief in them, vexed by the hard fiberglass.

Bathtubs are not made for prayer. My arms clung around her neck, waiting for the static to leave my legs. Closing my eyes, I tilted my chin toward my shoulder to expose my nubile throat to her mouth. Half moan, half whisper, I begged in her ear.

Notes of her amusement rang in my ears, soon followed by teeth sinking into my exposed vein. She sipped with delight the crimson spirit brewed by my heart. Greater a pain than any I had experienced, yet none more tolerable. I expected a stinging pain, but it was a deeper, aching one—like aftershocks of a blunt force. The chill when she grazed me, magnified a thousandfold. Opening my eyes, I saw blood mixing with water at our feet. The sight joined my pain and immobile bliss. My abdominal muscles contracted as my pussy pulsed out an orgasm—pulsing out through my skin, shivers, tremors. As soon as I rejoined my body, her fingers' delicate caress of my still-aroused shoulder brought me to orgasm a second time. A gush welled out between my weakening legs, indistinctly mingling with the water, spit, and blood.

The words of Porpentine echo in my mind: "When I look at a cis woman these days, the first thing I think is, I bet no one ever casually called her a rapist." Perhaps these words are too simplistic—transfeminine bodies have no monopoly on demonization. But her words echo deep in my gut. Who could be more predatory than the trans woman, when she *must* be severed from women's bathrooms and prisons, all the while 'womyn-born-womyn' remain comfortably unchallenged for their sexual violence? By the act of my birth, I have been made more predatory than predators.

I have long advertised myself as a bottom. Many mistake my conversational tone for dominance, but in the bedroom, there can be no mistake. *Yes daddy, please daddy, I will be a good girl.* If I were to strive for specificity, I would say I am a transfeminine bottom—that is, a switch with far too much emotional baggage to top. My fear of topping, my libidinal vertigo, is born out of trauma. So persistently have my body and naked existence been maligned, defamed as predatory, that the very idea of topping scares me. If I am predatory while submissive, what would be said if I donned dominance? What would be said if, though no wish of my own, I was to hurt others? A bad bottom may be boring, but a bad top spells trauma.

I recently found myself reading the words of Mary Daly and Janice Raymond—the literary canons of my transmisogynistic fusillade. Under their plume, I am a rapist both metaphorical and literal. Acts by my hand become an invasion, a violation of womanhood. Long before my birth, Mary Daly had already assigned predation to transfemininity. In *Gyn/Ecology*, in 1978, she foretold trans women's participation in the mythic paradigms of rapism. Her words are as violent as they are poetic:

> Mary Shelley displayed prophetic insight when she wrote Frankenstein, foretelling the technological fathers' fusion of male mother-miming and necrophilia in a boundary violation that ultimately points toward the total elimination of women.

To the theologian and supposed feminist, the act of altering my body is rape. The medical hands that held the scalpel, rapists. But as much as I may be an instrument, a creation of rape, the sympathy accorded to other progenies of sexual violence would never be extended to me. All may exceed the will and moment of their creation—unless you are trans. I, a monstrous creature of unnatural desires, am fixed by my birth. Transmisogynistic theology is an unforgiving hermeneutic.

Under the rule of two, Mary Daly sat as the kinder forebear. None was more famous, nor more spiteful in screed than her pupil Janice Raymond, Queen of TERFs. If the master saw transfeminine existence as an instrument of predation, the apprentice soon turned to qualifying trans women as sexual violators of the worst kind. No longer mere tools of an evil patriarchy, we were now rapists in our own right. Writing *The Transsexual Empire*, she explained:

> Rape, of course, is a masculinist violation of bodily integrity. All transsexuals rape women's bodies by reducing the real female form to an artifact, appropriating this body for themselves. However, the transsexually constructed lesbian-feminist violates women's sexuality and spirit, as well. Rape, although it is usually done by force, can also be accomplished by deception.

I can still recite the second sentence from memory, so broken am I by her words. Read the passage over a few times and tell me you do not hate yourself. No eloquence can capture the insidious knowledge that, as I trot down the sidewalk to fetch coffee a street over, those strolling around me believe the same— that I am a walking rape. Through metaphor comes literal ascription. Therein emerges an image of trans women as rapists in potentiality, as forthcoming rapists. Peeing is prohibited because, in this perverse image, I am always already a predator lying in wait.

They call me a metaphorical rapist to call me a literal one with greater ease soon thereafter. Once we are maligned as predators, inferring in us a propensity toward predation is simply natural.

Perhaps I could reply that rape is not a metaphor, *should not* be one. Metaphor offends the literal. But the reply misunderstands the foundational premise of transmisogynistic feminisms, an element that underwrites all its endeavors. You see, it is not that they fear transfemininity as a preface to rape. Rather, they believe metaphorical rape worse than literal rape. No rape is more depraved and ignominious to their mind than a metaphorical one. The wrongfulness of literal rape lies in instantiating the graver, original sin of metaphorical rape:

> Little more than a rape, indeed! What 'little more' is there to such an act, unless it is the total rape of our feminist identities, minds, and convictions? The transsexually constructed lesbian-feminist, having castrated himself, turns his whole body and behavior into a phallus that can rape in many ways, all the time. In this sense, he performs total rape, while also functioning totally against

women's will to lesbian-feminism.

Hearkening to Raymond's words, sprawled on the page for us to see, we can no longer see transfemininity as a mere predatory potential, as a mere propensity for violation. No. Transfemininity is the completed, perfected form of rape. Its Platonic ideal. Rape is not masculine—despite being often mistaken for such—but transfeminine. Through their despicable acts, all rapists share in the essence of transfemininity, like cultish parishioners receiving the Eucharist.

Transmisogyny cannot be understood without first understanding how the touch of transfemininity is viscerally constituted as a fate worse than rape by those who abhor us. Only in that knowledge was I finally able to understand their animosity toward such things as gender-concordant carceral housing—even as sexual offenders 'born-womyn' stood unquestioned, even as scores of female inmates experienced sexual assaults at the hands of other inmates. My rebuttals, my human rights, my science will never satisfy, for it is my existence that offends, not what I do with it. To Janice Raymond, *I am rape incarnate.* How, pray tell, am I supposed to avoid being fucked up by that knowledge?

Lover, know that any ambiguity will be interpreted against me. That's why I can foster no space for the messiness of sexuality, nor inhabit what I extend to others. I do not mean ignoring others' boundaries—though few relationships are free from crossings and punctures, however unintentional. No, I mean that I cannot afford the desire to act upon others. You want me to spank your ass red, fuck you raw. I want it too. I am familiar with these joys. But I can afford neither volition nor will. As soon as passivity leaves me, I am vulnerable—to being gaslit and ostracized, left for dead for the body I call mine. Social death over the vague sentiment that *I know we're not supposed to say this, but can't you feel that leftover male privilege and masculine energy?* This trench coat barely covering my masculinity and masculinist behavior is nothing more than a deceptive appearance of femininity. Sit in the thought before you excuse yourself of it; I have known too many so-called allies who partook in it. If not behind closed doors, then at the back of their unadmitting minds. The crazy trans woman syndrome, Morgan Page calls it.

Can you feel the tremor in my voice? Why I am so traumatized—can you feel it in your bones?

Faint-headed, I rested against the back of the tub while she dragged the lavender loofah against her lustrous skin. Perhaps my missing blood induced me to error, but it felt as though her hue had shifted,

alight by warmer, almost shimmering tones. "How
are you feeling," she inquired. I drowsily replied that
I was wonderful, eliciting a teasing giggle on her part.
She stepped out of the bathtub onto the mesh plastic
mat and pulled a light brown towel from the cast
iron towel rack on the wall of the tiled bathroom, the
one right above the radiator. After drying herself, she
carefully supported me out of my seat and guided
me to the antique radiator for me to lie against.
Taking the fluffier gray towel from the rack I was
resting on, she slowly patted me dry before taking me
in her arms. My arms around her neck, hers below
my knee and lower back, she carried us through the
corridor, living room, and into the bedroom, leaving
a trail of water as it dripped down my tousled locks
of hair. After resting my head against the lavender
sheets, she exited the room without a word.

Expecting her return, I flipped the switch of my
battery-powered faerie lights, springing to life little
dots of white against the shadow of my blanched
bedframe. Eve returned with a coffee mug—the black
one with 'witch's brew' inscribed in cursive across
the face—and, pausing for me to sit up, delivered it
to my lips. I cupped my palms to support the mug as
I guided its angle down to drink the lukewarm water;
she must not have known about the jug in the fridge.
While I drank, she deposited a small, yellow and red
envelope, no more than two by three centimeters,

on the bedside table. Switching hands, she dabbed a styptic pencil against my slowly coagulating neck to seal the cuts. Discarding the swab, she dragged her tongue in delight from below my clavicle upwards to the sealed imprints of her fangs, erasing the drying marks of blood from my neck.

Still faint, I slouched to my back and called her to me with a fan of the hand. She kissed my mouth and inserted her warm tongue between my colder lips, sliding and flicking around mine with unconsumed energy. Closing my mouth, I brought her head down to my shoulder and whispered for her to make me cum again. With an amused giggle, she pulled back and sat on the foot of the bed, atop the bunched sheets and flowery duvet. "No. I think you should make yourself orgasm." Reading the quizzical gaze in my eyes, she signaled a pause with her finger and, uncrossing her legs, rushed to the living room. Rummaging, I heard her open the doors of the built-in bookshelves. "I saw this coming in," she exclaimed from the other room as she peeked through the threshold of the *chambre à coucher*. In her hand, valiantly held up, I recognized the inscription across the fake leather cover. *Traduction Œcuménique de la Bible,* my childhood bible.

"Kneel." Obedient yet still frail, I sat sideways on my heels. Palpitations of arousal tussled in my stomach. Why had the sacrilegious text entered the fray? Sitting on the side of the bed, her torso slightly turned toward me, she cracked the spine open and searched with the knowing eyes of an apologetics scholar. The white of her eye glimmered as her finger stopped on a passage. Turning the book toward me, she recited: "This is my body, which is broken for you. This do ye in remembrance of me. This cup is the new covenant in my blood. This do as oft as you drink it, in remembrance of me." She traded her didactic tone for a raspy voice as she revealed her plans. "Play with yourself, and do not stop until the word of your pitiful Lord soaks with sin."

Blushing at her suggestion, I raised to my knees and let her lay the manuscript underneath me, the wrinkled spine keeping the pages open, soaking in the damp aroma of my engorged pussy. Under the intense glare of Eve's eye and bitten lip, I guided my right hand down my naked body, across my breast, patiently extending beyond my rusty pubis, and into the folds of my vulva. I noticed the scaling warmth at my lips, the unsubtle wetness of the entrance in which I slipped my middle finger before receding. I massaged my clitoris with my fingertip as my other fingers haughtily trailed behind, as though I was drinking from a teacup.

Electricity ran up from my clit into my arms

and legs, jolting an unintentional moan out of my nose. Holding my gaze to hers, I parted my fingers, pressing on either side of my clitoral hood. Lowering my other hand from behind my neck, I brought it to cusp my breast, clawing in the pain I wish she were inflicting upon my skin as she refused me her touch. "Good girl," she muttered in a reverberating tone.

Enlivened by her praise, aflame from her effortless control of my mind, body, soul, and spirit, I felt an imposing pressure build in my pelvic muscles, a drop of fluid flowing through my ducts as a warning. Leaning into the sensation, I relaxed my muscles. My entire body tensed up. My breath held itself instinctively. A few seconds later, the muscles contracted outwards, pushing, squirting a water-like fluid across the pages of the holy manuscript between my legs. I released my breathing, filling my throbbing head with the little blood left in me.

I could feel the orgasm radiating through my insides, across the depth of my skin, like waves of incandescent light mysteriously washing across the witching hour. Five, ten, I don't know how many seconds before I fell back on the bed. The pillow caught my head. After recovering my senses, I noticed the corner of the book pages digging against my thigh; noticed her pleased sigh, the depth of her laugh lines.

Taking the yellow and white wrapping from the nightstand, she revealed a double-edged razor blade—the same I use in my safety razor. "Shall I return the favor?" I was nervous. Blood arouses me, but I had only ever had my own. Hers was of another kind, an exquisitely monstrous one. Smiling behind my closed eyes, I softly nodded as she straddled over my hips. On her arm, I noticed an array of little white scars, brightened by their confluence. Cuts of alabaster against a skin that looked almost like pink salt next to it. Carefully holding the blade between two fingers and her thumb, she dragged its edge on top of her scar. Little dots of blood surfaced, slow at first, before merging into a line that rolled toward the inside of her forearm.

As I propped myself up on my elbows, she brought her arm to the side of my cheek. I turned my face toward her offering, relishing in the view of her blood—almost more maroon than crimson. Closing my eyes, I cleared the stream with my tongue before resting my mouth over the notch in her skin, as if to prevent an overflow. The taste was ineffable, with flavors like copper keys simmering in pomegranate juice and the sting of grapefruit against the flat of my tongue. The fluid melded with my saliva, penetrated my taste buds, coated the inside of my cheeks, the underside of my tongue, and the roof of my mouth. A musty, almost tangy taste lingered in the back of my throat after I swallowed. Like human blood, yet not quite. My mouth became numb, like I had just sipped a vial of lidocaine. A medicated rush; mellower, more of an opiate. My vision began to cloud, its field erased bit by bit by a swarm of honeybees protecting their queen—so ends my memory.

What would Jacques Lacan say about my fear of topping? I wonder. Or another psychoanalyst—I'm not picky, any vapid degradation will do. Beholden to a universal bisexuality that mistakes transitude for an overabundance of homosexual desire, some psychoanalytic minds would perhaps posit me anally fixated, but that won't do. I do not fear topping because I am a bottom; I am a bottom because I fear topping. Besides, if anything, I am orally fixated. *Alors, dites-moi, monsieur le psychanalyste, quelle est la source de ce vertige libidinal?*

Everything is pathological under the richness of psychoanalysis. Desiring abortion is no longer a natural happenstance wherein one's desired life clashes with the realities of pregnancies and parenting. No—that would be far too simple. Rather, it must be an anti-Œdipal attempt to kill the mother within. Running from the fumes of these scholastic conspiracy theories, we might decipher libidinal vertigo's psychic life as divestment from Œdipal guilt. Œdipus' tale is a loathsome one, a story of moral transgression that ends in the death of Laius, the suicide of Jocasta, and an Œdipus blinded from his own hand, having driven the pin of Jocasta's brooch through his blameful eyes. Œdipus is no enviable man. If Œdipal wishes are as irresolvable as they are incestuous and parricidal, guilt is a natural response. Perhaps, then, libidinal vertigo operates as divestment from that guilt, as a relinquishing of Œdipus' role in the psychosexual schema. A quintessentially psychoanalytic take—I cannot top because, for all my primordial Œdipal desires, I do not want to want to fuck my mom and kill my dad. Perhaps libidinal vertigo could even serve as a grand theory of transfemininity. In lieu of castration anxiety, penis anxiety and, via penis anxiety, castration envy. Libidinal vertigo is a divestment of irresolvable, predatory desires; psychoanalysis provides a wonderful interpretive companion to Mary and Janice. Which would be a deeply uncomfortable conclusion were it not for the fact that others seem perfectly comfortable in their incestuous desires. *Dis-moi, Jacques, comment va Émilie?*

Far from me the idea of proclaiming my speculations faithful to psychoanalytic thought. I am notoriously hostile to the discipline; I do not care for accuracy, nor faithfulness. Lacan can eat a cactus dick. No, but what I do affirm is that it's interesting to think about, betraying as it does one of the processes of guilt and torture that unfold in the deepest recesses of my mind, that chips away at my sense of self, erodes my *amour propre* speck by speck until my protective layers are stripped bare and trauma overtakes me. Stripped bare, behind the bells and whistles, dare I affirm this pseudo-psychoanalytic tale false? Am I not in some ways fleeing vestigial remnants of masculinity in myself by being a bottom? Am I not fearfully guarding against the predator that I was made to believe sleeps within?

Sometimes, when I lie in the crepuscular dark with only my tattoos and plush toys as company, I wonder if that fear of predation I have internalized, that libidinal vertigo, has formed part of my motivations for vaginomancy. Bottom surgery is to make a bottom by surgical means. Before the fated chop chop, I long favored a strap-on with flower-embroidered harness over my flesh penis. If the phallus is masculine, being able to take it off signals that masculinity does not adhere to me. Strapped on, I was devoid of inherent masculinity. Repudiation was always within reach, at most a few loosened buckles away. The thought scares me. It feels sacrilegious, something I should not dare admit even if it were truth. But why would it be wrong or blasphemous to fashion a surgical self from fear? May they whose gender is not made from scar tissue cast the first stone—for what is gender but scar tissue arranged in the shape of a self? Yet once the vapors of reason dissipate, the mere contemplation of that possibility feels forbidden, proscribed by the oracles of my contingent self. I could not admit it even if it were true. Of course, had I undergone vulvaworking in flight of masculinity, I would have soon realized that predation never inhered in the phallic form. Predation never inhered in phallic form. We may, as our favorite nun says, "cut off the most obvious means of invading women so that we seem non-invasive," but she will not be fooled. Besides, we all know I pursued vaginoplasty because women's clothing has no pockets. It was either that or learning sewing.

There are ideas that I would never for a minute believe, until one day I stop and ask myself: don't I? I do not believe myself predatory—but don't I? The presence of these rambling, rambunctious notions exhausts me, has worn bare the fabric that holds me together. Stigma is like a distributed denial-of-service attack. Reason does not matter—throw enough and you can bring anyone down. Lone transmisogynists reading my words, do not worry—should you fail, none torture me better than I do. A serpentine venom in my veins, the wound they inflicted cannot seem to heal, only fester.

Dominance, topping—they are no more predatory than anything else that can be misused. These ascriptions of predatoriness are arbitrary; they disparage, defame, injure. There is a certain kindness in topping. An attentiveness that belies its associations with predation. A gentleness I wish to return to my devoted partners—I know the desire that sears their soul; I know that to fulfill it is holy. Is there not a sliver of divinity in the blushing cheek of a lover, a simulacrum of our savior's blood allowing us to partake in sacrament? To top is to care for someone's needs above your own—is that not self-sacrifice? Fellow creature, how dare I claim the mantle of the monster if I do not dare live the exquisitely monstrous desires that are my own?

One is not born, but rather becomes, a bottom. I don't know how to heal the gaping wound transmisogyny has left in my chest. To fully embrace my monstrosity is but a dream. Janice Raymond's words spin in my head, torturing me. "All transsexuals rape women's bodies by reducing the real female form to an artifact, appropriating this body for themselves." Existence is shame.

But as I write, other words take their place in my mind. Ones I heard but the other day. Aching words, bringing tears to my eyes, these eyes that have all but forgotten how to weep. "She was lying then, and the echo of her voice may sound like your own now, but she is still lying." Mending words, if only I could believe them.

Perhaps the wound is not yet a scar. Perhaps there can still be healing.

When will we be allowed to be deficient, messed up, terrible?

Because honestly fuck having to be nice, sensible girls who don't do problematic things.

Cisters sure as hell don't get beat out of bathrooms for thinking the dress makes the woman.

Trans liberation means your gender can just be forced feminization fetish taken too far.

It also means you're allowed to be trans because you're just too fucking gay to be cis.

It means a lot of things.

Not all those things are savory or respectable.

Everyone else gets to build their gender out of scar tissue.

Everyone else gets to just be fucked up.

Why not us?

A Law Clerk Comes in Ottawa

"Hold it." I raised my eyes to look at them. I could feel the flame growing ever warmer as it burned through the matchstick, thinning it to a flimsy string of charcoal. Marie's eyes glared at me from the lounging chair as they petted Claire's head resting on their lap. Hearing Marie's command, Claire perked up to look at me. We were both kneeling on the floor—she at Marie's feet, I at the coffee table upon which rested the tea candle I had been asked to light. I deviated my gaze from Marie's, turning back to the half-burnt match. The flame was still far from my skin, but its invisible, radiating heat was already at my fingers, nearing my pain threshold.

"Hold it." Titillated by her order, I did not want to let go but knew I would soon. As the flame bit into the tips of my index and thumb, my reflexes took over and I dropped the match onto the candleholder.

A sensation of fear flowed to my extremities, fear of the punishment she would bestow upon me for my transgression—or was it trepidation?

"Good girl." The murky, oily fright was suddenly washed off by the electricity running from the tips of my fingers into my stomach, sitting there like the leftover buzz from touching a capacitor with your thumb. Marie is a fair and kind ruler. A pleased smile on their face, their murky brown eyes fell to the candle atop its wooden holder before slowly rising to meet my body. Huffing a muted chuckle, an order parted their lips. "Stand up and undress for us."

I was nervous—of course I was nervous. I could feel the sweat coat the palms of my hands. I wiped them on my dress just like my mom told me not to. After saluting the sword lesbian in front of the building, I had announced myself to the employee entrance and, after being checked for weapons— though they forgot my wit—I was brought to this room. A large room with wooden walls of tawny port color, illuminated by two large windows on the back wall. Anxious, I had gotten up from the central table and walked to the bookshelves built into the walls. The room was mainly filled with old copies of the Dominion Law Reports, but one of the bookshelves carried books about apex courts. Running my fingers across the familiar spines, I paused at a gold-trimmed copy of Justice William Rehnquist's *The Supreme Court: How It Was, How It Is*. Waiting for my turn to speak to the judges, I wondered the same about our northern court. How *is* it? Will I get to know?

Becoming the first openly transfeminine clerk at the Supreme Court of Canada would be a great honor. Interviewing for the position was surreal. Yet, at the same time… what in the ever-living fuck was I doing here? In this temple to solemnity, which a fragment buried deep in my soul loathes so. I feared that even if I stood a chance, I would merely end up disallowed from myself. Drafting memos on tax law instead of writing sex jokes in the footnotes of peer-reviewed papers. Solemnly deliberating the minutiae of doctrine instead of showing colleagues my tits. Respectability is a slippery slope.

I smirked at the bookshelf. Was I not, not so long ago, guest lecturing topless at Osgoode Hall? I was. I taught *Québec c. Anglsberger*. Taught how the judge, agitated by the psychiatrist expert, ruled sexuality oxymoronic with transitude. The plaintiff Dame D was a proper transsexual, soberly dressed and respectably employed. To discriminate against her was an affront to civility. But sex workers? Or those scandalously dressed since, for the judge, they were all the same? No. *They* can only be transvestites, sexual deviants. So I taught, in boots and lace panties. Three students wrote reflection papers on my tits—two good, and one by a man. Earth is for the shameless.

There is no worse sin against respectability than having a sexuality. For all its talks of freedom of expression, academia is deeply sex negative. It tolerates not those whose desires are carnal, whose desires are anything other than Platonic. Academic sex-shaming is well suited to dominant interests, to those who never had to learn they have a body. As universities become ever-more unaffordable, marginalized students are disproportionately turning to sex work only to find themselves rejected *a priori* from academia, as though soiled by cardinal sin. My hat, I tip thee. What an inventive way of casting off the oppressed without naming them. Be racist all you want—that is forgivable—but sharing nudes on the internet? I can hear the pearls being clutched. It matters not that none are hurt by it—quite the contrary, my nudes are delectable.

Sometimes, I am surprised that I have yet to be excommunicated from the legal profession and its attendant academe. I have spent many days in fear that the overtly sexual content on my social media would come back to haunt me, would disqualify me from the ranks of the professoriate. A contingent of dastardly professors appears to be attempting to banish me from academia. Yet for little more than being transfeminine; nothing so lofty as my unrepentant sexuality. I wish I were vain enough to believe they will not succeed. I wish I were naïve enough to believe my colleagues and mentors would protect me, despite my sparring with the boundaries of Victorian propriety. It is there that sexuality comes back into the fray. It makes me indefensible. If you raise the cost of allyship by breaching prudish mores, you soon find yourself without allies. Sexuality may not alone spell my doom, but by adding itself to my abhorrent self, it weakens the natural defenses that already crumble around me. Will I let them wear me down, beat me into submission? Only time will tell. I don't think I would love this kind of submission quite as much.

If I clerked for a judge in the highest of judicial instances, my Twitter would have to die. They must not have found it, for me to even have an interview. I giggle thinking about the sixty-nine joke hidden in the full version of my writing sample. "*The term 'third gender' should be avoided, as different non-binary identities are distinct genders. Why third and not sixty-ninth? That sounds way more fun…*"

As a clerk, I would have to stop showing everyone my tits. I would have to desist from being so *horny on* *main*. After spending decades of my life wandering the thick fogs of the null hypothecis, there are few things I fear as much as losing myself—again. In these halls, would I join the subdued pearl-clutching elites of the world, ripe for the guillotine? I fear as much. Perhaps I can place in myself a secret mark of my rebellion. In that symbol, place all my hope; dare try and hold onto who I am. Perhaps I could sign documents with my initials. *Fap*—fap all over the chamber.* Sexuality, indelibly attached to my name. Restraints were never my *forte*.

Have you ever gotten slutshamed by a judge? With just a bit of luck, I might soon.

Tilting the flame, Claire poured a couple beads of wax on her exposed thigh. My naked body on the peach bedsheets as a backdrop, she turned to Marie and presented the candle with a nod. My arms extended above my head, a shiver coursed through them, raising the glittery blonde hairs on their ends. Marie shook their head and walked around to the head of the bed. They crouched over the edge to kiss my upside-down lips, leaving behind a smell of watermelon bubblegum. Leaving my lips, Marie pushed themselves up using my arms

---

* My full name is Florence Ashley Paré. Yes, *on purpose*.

as leverage, pinning me down. Gazing up toward Claire as I playfully fought against my restraints—a single hand, barely more than two fingers, wrapped around my wrists—Marie invited her service as my lascivious torturer.

A moment of fright. I could feel my heartbeat; yes, faster, but, especially, deeper—a rumbling drum. My skin began to tingle from the beads of sweat forming in my pores. The chill of evaporation only further contrasted with the heat I dreaded from the pooling paraffin. Casting a circular motion, a couple feet above my exposed breasts, Claire poured a filament of wax on the surface of my skin. The initial touch burned like splatters of cooking oil—only a fraction of a second. A fraction of a second before my flustered nervous system adjusted to the sensation and settled into the comforting warmth of a pastel peach sunburn after a long day reading in the shade. The wax set almost immediately, arranging itself into a glistening bouquet of hydrangeas. A bead of wax trickled down the side of the candle and dripped onto my areola, as if to tease me with the whispers of its boundless pleasures.

Freeing my wrists, Marie disappeared for a moment. In their absence, dashes of wax continued to periodically rouse my senses. Claire lurched over me, wearing only her green boybriefs, her lavender hair wrapped in a messy bun. Soon returned with a strapless strap-on in hand, Marie lifted their leg onto the bedframe and effortlessly slid the bulbar end inside their vagina. At their approach, Claire set the candle down on the nightstand, blowing a soothing aroma of soot into the air, and let herself fall to her side. Lying next to me, she raised her hips to remove her panties and threw them playfully at Marie.

So I'm sitting there, crayola jizz on my titties, taking in Marie's ethereal silhouette atop me, their purple cock casting a foreboding shadow on my belly. Their unfazed, pensive demeanor; their elvish ears; a surgical scar dividing the lower half of their breasts, as though the seams of a cyborg— together, a dreamlike aura. Coming to my senses, I noticed Claire's hand clasping mine; we, on our backs, returning a mesmerized gaze unto Marie as if surrendering to a trans/humanist deity.

Carefully, Marie penetrated me with the lubricated strap-on as Claire watched on in envy, absent-mindedly stroking her soft dick. I raised my hips to adjust the angle of entry as the large silicone cock stretched my body around itself. A primal, uncontrolled moan left my lips as Marie turned the motor on, sending a jolt through my vaginal walls. A ripple of pleasure shattered through my entrails, making my abs contract as though under an electric shock. Three seconds; one, two, three—before I felt the moisture of an orgasm take over my pussy, my entire body shaking in debilitating pleasure. I *have* to get myself one of those.

Turning their pleased eyes upon the writhing Claire, Marie coated their finger in saliva. They lowered their hand to tease Claire's taint and thighs before, so soon after, inserting their wet finger in her ass. I felt her hand tighten around mine. A finger inside her, a cock inside me, our voices joined in a song of unity and harmony, a melodic expression of the secret fire lit in our midst.

"We don't usually let people enter this way," she told me, swinging the doors open. "But I find it most impressive." We were standing on the threshold of the courtroom, behind the judges' bench, looking down at the empty lectern. Little white notepads watermarked with the Cormier emblem sat in front of each of the nine seats. The room was strikingly small compared to what I had imagined. Unassuming, unimpressive. It looked so much larger—grander— on video. A matter of perspective.

This room is meant for sober contemplation. It glorifies the mind, praises wit—not virtue, not emotion. There is no justice in these halls, only law.

Our education, under the name of Socratic method, plays devil's advocate for a pretty penny. Law school is a boot camp for neoliberalism. There were our judges trained. *Bullshit.* I want to jump on the desks and strip for the gallery. I want to desecrate this altar of prurience. Maybe have an orgy atop the counsel tables.

Sex in the courtroom—an idea that would abhor judges far more than the injustices that have, time and time again, been dealt by the stroke of their pen. Doubtless I would be arrested by the mounted police contingent in the basement. A clever name, the *mounted* police. As though they wore little red uniforms as they ceremonially rode horses through the halls of the court. The name makes them sound far nicer than they are, with their assault rifles and bulletproof vests, contemptuously marching the corridors. Sex in an empty room—worse than colonialism, capitalism, patriarchy, and white supremacy.

Standing at the lectern as if pleading before the judges, I pondered upon sex's offense to society. Fear of sex is inscribed on the very surface of Christianity's creation myth—a fear of sex as a source of power. Through carnal knowledge, Eve found in herself the strength to stand up against her ruthless creator and demand her due. For this transgression, she was cast out of paradise. Courts, earthly enforcers of divine supremacy, now disavow her weapons—too strong were they. Sex sowed the seeds of a revolt against tyrannical rule. Its power must be suppressed.

To them, we are not living and breathing lovers. We are ghosts in the machine. In his *Meditatio VI*, René Descartes infamously stipulated one of the foundations of modern life: "So it is certain that I am really distinct from my body and can exist without it." The body can be neglected. It matters not. Its wants are base. It knows nothing. You will be asked to neglect your emotional and personal lives, neglect your boundaries—no, you cannot go pee, change your pad, or have a body that distracts boys. To have a body is the original sin. Sex is the sin among sins, reminding us of our flawed nature as feeling beings in a world that wants us ethereal. But in the pursuit of ethereality, we were made undead. All the easier to manage for our corporate overlords.

The courtroom thrives in patriarchal, racial capitalism. And so, it degrades the body and elevates the mind. Capitalism works best when bodily needs are unacknowledged and physical labor devalued. Bodies stand in the way of infinite production. In the halls of the law, feeling is disavowed. Its carpet is red with the lifeblood of those it intellectualizes beyond recognition. The highest court in the land is one where only lawyers speak, sparring with quick tongues and tamed hearts. The mastery of mind over body is lauded as human perfection. The greater the distance from the world, the better the academic, the better the judge. Embodied knowledge can only come forth if it is tamed, turned into abstraction through secondhand metamorphosis. Objectivity, free speech. Not perception, compassion.As a judge, a lawyer, a politician, a scholar, I would be afraid. Sexuality is not base. It is brilliant. Eroticism taught me to listen to the sentiments in the deepest recesses of my skin, in all its twists and all its folds. It taught me to acknowledge these desires. It taught me that my needs deserved meeting. It taught me that I deserved love, that I deserved to love myself on the terms I chose. The erotic's shine on my body—that is how I realized I was trans.

The body is an epistemology. Its pains and joys are not mere incidents of existence. They are teachers. I have not succeeded in my craft *despite* horniness but because of it. My extravagance, my passion, and my creativeness spring forth from embodied sensations, from the erotic recognition of my and others' primordial worth. None disposable under the pretext of pursuing higher truths. The body is an epistemology, and that epistemology is revolutionary. Was this not the manifesto of queerdom?

Being queer is 'grass roots' because

we know that everyone of us, every body, every cunt, every heart and ass and dick is a world of pleasure waiting to be explored. Everyone of us is a world of infinite possibility. We are an army because we have to be. We are an army because we are so powerful. And we are an army of lovers because it is we who know what love is. Desire and lust, too. We invented them. We come out of the closet, face the rejection of society, face firing squads, just to love each other! Every time we fuck, we win.

In *The Uses of the Erotic*, Audre Lorde traced in her Black lesbian desires the source of a revolutionary power. For the erotic sits in us as "an internal sense of satisfaction to which, once we have experienced it, we know we can aspire." Bodily epistemology, a source of power and information, the provocative force of true feeling. Her prophetic words resonate in me as I read them for the umpteenth time:

For having experienced the fullness of this depth of feeling and recognizing its power, in honor and self-respect we can require no less of ourselves. ... Our erotic knowledge empowers us, becomes a lens through which we scrutinize all aspects of our existence, forcing us to evaluate those aspects honestly in terms of their relative meaning within our lives. And this is a grave responsibility, projected from within each of us, not to settle for the convenient, the shoddy, the conventionally expected, nor the merely safe.

Revolutionary thought begins when we realize that the ills and wells of the body are generative. That the body is not secondary, not an inconvenience to be suppressed as we pursue unearthly ideals. It comes from the realization that the rational economic mind is no rationality of ours. Abstraction is a flawed epistemology. Ours must be one of love.

Sleeping with Marie and Claire was my first threesome. It occurred the day after the phone call offering me a position at the Supreme Court. The phone call I received a few hours after my interview as I stepped out of the shower naked and wet. To call our debauchery a reward would distort its truth. Moreso, it was a ritualistic thank, an offering to the sexuality and embodied knowledge that guides my pace through life. A reminder of what I cannot forget, of what I cannot lose. I am not saying that sending nudes from the bathroom before a hearing would make me a better clerk, but there is no substitute for having a body. The erotic cannot be felt secondhand. Wouldn't you be afraid of it, too?

My gender is tired
it is old
and leathery
it has scars and crow's feet

One day I'll trade it in for a new one
like this one replaced the old
when I noticed it didn't fit anymore

Or maybe it's not my gender
that's tired
maybe it's me
tired from reading the comment sections
of my news feed
It feels like all I am is my gender
I can't feel where it ends and where I begin

My gender is tired
it is old and leathery
or maybe that's just me

Daydreams of an Apocalypse

Her hand caresses my neck as she leans into a kiss just below my ear. Her lips grazing the duvet at the back of my neck send a shiver through my shoulder. I quickly save my file with a few keystrokes and swivel my chair around to look at her. I have been writing for hours, lost in the grief of words. She smiles at me, as if to welcome me back to the land of the living, the un-dead. I smile back.

"Come, I have something to show you." She extends her hand for me to take. Her delicate nails are painted raven black, in inspiration of me. I hold onto her ring and pinkie fingers as she briskly skips to the bedroom. She swings the door open and shakes her fists in excitement before her creation. "Tada!"

A paisley bedsheet hangs from the corner of the bed, upwards to the bookshelf—tucked under heavy books—and back down toward the dressing table. A tower fan holds up the fabric at the midpoint between the shelf and table, fastened with a clothespin. Inside the structure, two stacked duvets mime a makeshift bed. The one on the bottom is uncovered, showing its beige white stained with faint rings of sweat. The one on top is the color of charcoal, embroidered with silvery leaves in the shape of rounded hexagrams. A blanket fort to envelop our bodies, to keep us away from the world's prying eyes.

I giggle and throw my arms around her neck, kissing her in thanks. Breaking our embrace, she closes the door, goes to sit cross-legged on the duvets, and beckons me inside with her outstretched arms. A warmth crosses my breast as I bathe my eyes in her serene beauty. I cannot tell apart the light of the overcast sun from that of the fairy lights hung around the ceiling. The shade of bluish pink highlights the freckles of our forearms and gives my hair a copper tone, at once deeper and brighter. Crossing arms at my waist, I remove my dress and kneel in front of her, laying a kiss on her parted lips. She kisses me back passionately; in her breath, hints of a warm strawberry compote, the soothing scent of a summer's eve.

In one fluid motion, I turn around and sit with my back against her. She rests her arms around my chest. Closing my eyes, her skin feels almost like velvet against mine. My skin craves hers still, the inexhaustible longing of pandemic days. I inhale deeply through my nose and exhale through my mouth the aches of my day. Cloistered between the fragile walls around us, our world is small. Tiny and peaceful, our misery forgotten like a nightmare shortly after dawn.

The spirit within me wearies. I see each day pass another by, forever in want of change. I see the skies fall by a few inches each day. The latches holding it have ruptured under the weight of our selfishness. A suffocating smoke fills my lungs. I feel the nausea, the dizziness. I don't write this as mere hyperbolic prose; I often have to lay in bed, a pit in my stomach, at unpredictable times of the day because I am scared shitless by what tomorrow will bring and struggle to imagine anything further away.

Is it depression? Perhaps, and yet. How do I fight a despair that seems so reasonable? A few years ago, my mother asked for my wishes for the new year. I told her candidly of my wish not to get stabbed. Neo-Nazis armed with knives had been hanging around queer bars in Montreal. Usually optimistic to a fault, I saw on my mother's face a nod of resigned agreement. My answer to her had been half-considered, not quite in jest yet not quite earnest. In truth, only with her response did I feel the full weight of my fears. Little has changed since; as I write, far-right rags have had a few good weeks of running articles targeting me for saying something about how gendering animals normalizes bioessentialism. Their comments, an ode to my inhumanity. I should stop reading them, but I have a perverse fascination with others' revulsion. Maybe if I acquaint myself with their contempt, it can no longer take me by surprise. But worry not—for every person who wishes me dead, two will put pronouns in their email signature. Biweekly declarations of empty support as I read the morning news of yet another frantic attempt to excise trans lives from society.

Hearken unto me, fellow creatures. We, trans communities, are not the only ones targeted—far from it. Society is imploding. Witness the dismantling of the welfare state and the semblance of any social net. The ruthless exploitation of land and workers, the brutalities freely dispensed to those Black and Indigenous people who dare exist before the eye of a militaristic police. Over the horizon, if you squint a bit, you can see the downfall of civil and human rights at the hands of demagogues and populists. And if that was not enough, our little grassy ship through space is on fire. A climate crisis, approaching with unshaken determination. Choose your poison; there is no happy ending.

Once, I had hoped that my dearest communism would arrive in time to save us from despondency. Alas, I fear the demise of capitalism will not come to pass. Overcoming greed, endless consumption, and so-called merit; abolishing poverty and inequality—pipe dreams from more naïve days of mine. The promise of revolution is not one I see in the future. Not in time to save humanity from the climate apocalypse. Only barely have we sacrificed our comforts to survive a pandemic. Survive… at least seven million did not. How foolish would it be to think ourselves capable of collecting our forces and beating back planetary warming, so affectively distant it is, against the prodigious authority of capital, forever hungering for its own expansion.

Those who resist with a voice loud enough that power takes notice will be met with violence unbecoming. Among the greatest threats to racial capitalism was the Black Power Movement. And so was Fred Hampton assassinated by agents of the state as his girlfriend lay in bed next to him. Some fifty-two years ago, his death—revolutionary movements no longer pose a threat. The brutalities of the police against those who protest its violence are for its own amusement and delight. The police is now militarized, and the military equipped with hi-tech toys of mass destruction. Never has the disparity been greater between the soldiers of capital and the people. If there was ever a time for revolutionary movements to succeed, it lies in the past.

In truth, conspicuous violence rarely needs be resorted to. Capitalism has perfected the ability to quash threats to its sovereignty. The tools of ideology turn the pressure valves, let off just enough steam for the pipe not to explode. Leaders and elites at the margins can be assimilated and brought into the fold, dead or alive. Their revolutionary thought, if they have any, can be sterilized and turned into a marketing strategy. If all else fails, give them a professorship. In 1917, Vladimir Lenin wrote about how great revolutionaries were made 'hip' among the liberal elite:

> After their death, attempts are made to convert them into harmless icons, to canonize them, so to say, and to hallow their names to a certain extent for the 'consolation' of the oppressed classes and with the object of duping the latter, while at the same time robbing the revolutionary theory of its substance, blunting its revolutionary edge and vulgarizing it.

There is nothing worse for a movement than its co-optation by capital. Capitalism has had some hundred years since to polish its ideological stratagems. Their sophistication is without rival. Martin Luther King Jr. has become an idol of white liberals. Seamlessly, quotes from Malcolm X are deployed to criticize radical Black voices. The legacies of Marsha P. Johnson and Sylvia Rivera are turned into soundbites before our eyes, to be used by reformist trans movements and their middle-class ex-military leaders. Today, even Justin Trudeau is an intersectional feminist—taking a knee at a Black Lives Matter event and tweeting his sorrow at the mass graves of Indigenous children just before signing off on another pipeline or appealing a court ruling that requires his government to finance healthcare and education for Indigenous youth. Oh and of course, how mightily unconcerned does he seem about the lack of clean drinking water on reserves. But don't worry—he *gets* it.

Radicalism has become little more than a spectacle. A brand, a marketing strategy, an *aesthetic*. Like punk when I was young; all it took was a spiky belt and an album with the parental advisory tag—no matter that this little frenchie kid could not understand any of the lyrics. Radicalism is no longer a matter of feeling, compassion, or commitment, but one of appearances. I do not mean to deny the profound affect that underlies the unyielding pledge of many leftists. But you cannot organize a revolution if you do not know which of your comrades will remain at your side past the first sign of strife. With hashtags and Pepsi ads, we have been disarmed. O hope, how I wish you could still be mine to bear.

> Je suis une cage d'oiseau
> Une cage d'os
> Avec un oiseau
>
> L'oiseau dans ma cage d'os
> C'est la mort qui fait son nid

So begins my favorite poem by Hector de Saint-Denys Garneau, perhaps the only one I know. I am a birdcage. A cage of bone, with a bird. The bird in my bone cage—it is death making its nest. The poem reminds me of *Belzébuth* from *Dehors novembre*.

Every so often, I wake up crying from a dream of pregnancy. Crying, because I will never experience a burgeon of life taking form by my stomach, growing in the nook between my ribs and pelvis. I would be stunning with a baby bump. But on this wretched earth, my prayers are being reshaped, torn into gratitude. Never will I be the cause of another's existence. Perhaps it is a blessing, so beset am I already with worries for the younglings in my life. Death sounds peaceful—a thought I caught myself thinking a few days ago, for the first time in a decade.

How do you live in a world that can never be repaired? How do you resist when you are too exhausted to dream of a future? Far too often have I daydreamed of giving up, of fleeing to the forest, to live in a small cabin of pine and cypress hidden in the depths of a valley. In flowing dresses and crowns of flower wreaths, there to dance barefoot on the twigs and needles with my girlfriend, in between gathering berries and logging wood. An impotent dream, I must concede. Between boredom, guilt, and the early onset of osteoporosis should I dare renounce pharmaceuticals, I wouldn't last long. Outside, November—I prefer the city.

Not long ago, I began to play with an idea in my head. What if I conceived of activism as a palliative endeavor, rather than one guided by a utopic end? In palliative care, living past illness is no longer the goal. Something of a ritual, and much of a prayer. Its goal is to ease pains, like a balm after the sun; to cultivate comfort and love among the suffering. How do you help in a world of fire? What do you do when you run out of water? Cuddle and fuck. Aren't the flames pretty? Let them set the mood. Suck dick. Eat pussy. Build a bookcase. Write a poem for the friend you're crushing on. Kiss your lover under a rain that pours like nails from heaven; leave your damp clothes on the floor and shower with your bodies held together for warmth like mousebirds. Love one another—because the world sure fucking won't. Palliative activism is a joyful or, at least, content pessimism. Maybe even an optimistic fatalism. Or fatalistic optimism—I don't know what words mean anymore. If we are doomed to suffer, maybe we can ensure that there will be love among the suffering.

An outgrowth of my hopelessness, in palliative activism I would give up my hopes for revolution and justice, replacing them with comfort in the now-and-then. Like revolutionary struggle, its progenitor, palliative demands change—yet its demands are not in the hopes of crafting one day a just future but to reduce the pain and injustices that so many carry unto the end of days. If you are still capable of hope, then hope—I envy you. But I must figure out how to go on when weariness cuts you bare. No, I don't want to give up on systemic change, nor turn away from justice—I want to hold and cradle them in my arms, warm them, hold them close to my heart—but I know this won't do anymore. Not without faith. But perhaps I can hold onto them if I approach with a mind toward harm reduction rather than a teleological attitude that besets me with unkindness.

To reduce suffering and hold each other in kindness and care is still an activism. Giving up cannot be palliative; nor can liberalism. We do not diminish misery—at least not well—by helping only those most privileged among us. Even if the revolution never comes, liberal reformism cannot be squared with the materialism of palliative activism. A wish for life, not formalities, not rights for the rich marginals. And besides, you and I both know that there is no fun in kissing up to the powers that be. Their asses aren't that soft. Pleasure lies in the fight. May the bridges we burn offer warmth and comfort—we must imagine Sisyphus happy.

What would I do differently if this decade were my last? My eyes set on revolution, I have often found anger in my bones and the kindness disappeared from my voice. Too often have I sought to be right rather than kind. Too often have I lacked kindness toward myself, wallowing in the infinite guilt of... perhaps I could have done more. More, and perhaps we could have had our revolution.

Wishing revolution has erected a barrier against my enjoyment of the world that remains. *Feu* Lauren Berlant called these hindering desires 'cruel optimism.' Cruel optimism appears when the object of your desire—say, communism—becomes an obstacle to your happiness and flourishing. Cruel is the optimism that seeks happiness yet inhibits it.

My palliative activism is a bittersweet response

to the cruel optimism of revolution. It cultivates the ephemeral bubbles of love and community. It invites us to surrender to the love and care we *can* foster. It holds space for being wrong, for being flawed, for redemption. I have been unforgiving of imperfection, though negligible its harms can sometimes be, for want of revolution. But the revolution is not at stake; I am no longer able to dream of perfection. How about we cut ourselves and each other some slack? How about we refuse to let idealism get in the way of our present needs, present loves, present communities? We are not disposable.

Palliative activism begins where grief turns to wisdom, and wisdom to care. It carves its roots in the (post-)erotic entanglements of anarchic love, surges from those abandoned moments where we dare care for the wounded bird within ourselves. Because refusing the banality of cruelty, refusing to be worn bare, refusing to do violence unto each other—these may damn well be the closest we will come to revolution.

Maybe I am too far gone to hope anymore. But, for solace, there may still be hope.

"Would our friends be there?" The dusk has set some time ago. The fairy lights have turned to dark purple. Our bodies intermingled, we are talking about the end of world, the apocalypse. A meteor crashing down to extinguish us as it did the dinosaurs. Or nuclear bombs hijacked by an artificial superintelligence. Or maybe a tentacled cosmic horror craving the magma at the planet's core. Varied as the scenarios may be, the plan is the same. Sitting on two sofa chairs in the middle of the empty street, we would hold hands and sip *nectar d'or* whisky as grandiloquent bells mark the expiry of human suffering.

"Of course, we would invite them! Wouldn't it be a wonderful day for a community barbecue?" I smile with my reply. Being with our loved ones means more bad apocalypse jokes. Delightful. "We could haul the grill to the middle of the street, behind the sofas, and make some burgers and hot dogs. Can you see it when you close your eyes, all warm and sunny against the smell of humidity? But we shouldn't forget sunscreen." She tightens her arms around me. I can hear the tremors of her heart through her breast. "I don't want this to end," she whispers.

I raise my head and kiss her chin. A distance shy of her lips, I prop myself up on my elbows to press my mouth against hers. She hangs softly onto my lower lip as if telling me not to go, telling *us* not to go. My tongue slides against the enamel of her teeth, in the gap between her lips and mine. I mirror her loving bite, holding onto her bottom lip, returning her message. Withdrawing from her mouth, I stare into her eyes, trying to decipher the messages hidden in her dark pupils. My heart swells three sizes at her grace. I can feel it pressing against my ribs. "I am not going anywhere."

Resting my head back on her chest, I rummage through the duvets. Having found what I was looking for, I turn off the fairy lights and whisper good night. The thunder rages in the distance; she tightens her arms around me. The gloom in my heart has dissipated. I doubt I will ever wake up to a better world. But falling asleep in her arms, that doesn't feel so bad. Maybe next time, I'll be a bird.

May the bridges we burn offer warmth and comfort.
May the bridges we burn light the way.

Florence Ashley

Florence Ashley (they/them/that bitch) is a transfeminine professor of law and bioethics at the University of Alberta. A prolific transdisciplinary researcher, Florence has mesmerized many academic fields with their incisive style and irreverent footnotes. Their first book was more boringly titled *Banning Transgender Conversion Practices: A Legal and Policy Analysis*. When not engaged in research or teaching, Florence enjoys speaking French, oversharing on social media, and getting railed in a sundress.